nurture

To
Anthony,
without whose support and encouragement none of this would have been possible.

nurture

Notes and recipes from Daylesford Farm

Carole Bamford

EBURY PRESS

CONTENTS

9	Introduction

DAYLESFORD

24	The Creamery
32	The Bakery
42	Our Animals
52	The Market Garden
62	The Farm Shops
70	The Old Spot
78	The Cookery School
84	Daylesford Garden
90	Daylesford Cottages
98	Bamford
112	The Wild Rabbit

SEASONAL RECIPES AND CELEBRATIONS

118	Spring
150	Summer
186	Autumn
224	Winter

WELL-BEING

274	The Haybarn Spa
295	End note
296	Acknowledgements
299	Index

INTRODUCTION

I begin every day by taking my dogs for a walk around the farm. The dairy's milking team will already be hard at work and I'll usually see a few heads among the rows of vegetables or fruit trees, lifting or trimming or tending to our market garden. And as I look around, I am still so immensely proud of what I see. What began as a desire to make a small difference to the health and future of our planet, and to feed my family in a better way, has grown from a collection of empty barns and bare fields to become Daylesford.

This book tells a little of the story and shares the beliefs and ideas that have led to Daylesford becoming what it is today; how and why I started along a path to lead a more conscious life and how that path continues to teach and challenge and fill me with joy every day. But it also celebrates the work of so many others. I am very fortunate to be surrounded by the most brilliant team, who are as passionate and committed to Daylesford's philosophy as I am. Above all they are driven by the same desire to share the work that we do as widely as possible. I have a vision but my team are the experts – they are the ones who make it all happen.

My hope is that you might take even just a little of what you are about to read and be inspired to make a difference too. I believe it's not just doing a good deed, it's a responsibility. We're custodians of our land, our soil, our bodies and minds, and our precious planet and I think we can all make small changes to live in a more mindful way, to take care of them and strive to leave our world in a better state than we find it. Cooking and eating well were central to my childhood. I'm a child of the 1950s and I know that has had a huge part to play in shaping my life. I grew up in a time when food was still rationed so we had to make the most of what we had and much of the way I do things today is simply how we lived back then – we looked after things; we looked after ourselves and we looked after the land.

When I think back to that time it reminds me to be very grateful for what I have today. So many of us have lost sight of where our food comes from but food has a real value and I worry that sometimes we forget that. We've lost that connection between field and fork – the how and why our food comes to be on our plates. We sit down to meals often without a second thought about what we're eating and without sensing or savouring the flavours and ingredients. Mealtimes have always been very important to me but even more so from the time I became a mother. As well as being the time to nurture and nourish our bodies well, meals are an opportunity to bring my family together, to spend time celebrating and enjoying our food together and acknowledging the work and care that have gone into creating it. I like to make an effort with the table setting at mealtimes – to set a scene and make it look special – and I love seeing others enjoy that.

Farming was very different back then too. We didn't use chemicals and pesticides

because we didn't have them. There were only small farms where everything was free-range and it was organic by nature. Then in the late 1960s and 70s came this big push towards progressive agriculture – big machinery and huge farms whose sole aim was to reap as much from their crops and livestock as they possibly could, whatever the means. Farming was no longer about working with nature's natural rhythms and timescale; it was all about speeding things up. The hedgerows were pulled out to create more space for the fields, wildlife and bees lost their natural habitat, and soil health and plant diversity were sacrificed in the race to produce as much as possible. It seemed like such a good idea, yet what is clear now is that it wasn't sustainable – it was instant gratification in return for years of damage and loss.

When I married, we lived on a farm in Staffordshire and it was there that I was first struck by the idea that things needed to change. Starting to farm organically wasn't a decision for me. Once I'd learned about what was being done to our countryside, our food and our planet there was simply no way back – I couldn't go back.

It was a very hot summer – the heatwave of 1976 – when I was in the garden with my first baby Alice and noticed that my newly-planted roses were beginning to wilt. I could hear these big machines spraying something so I went to see the farmer next door to ask him about it and he told me they were spraying Roundup. I didn't like the sound of that, and I could smell it; it was everywhere. I learned later that Roundup is a strong herbicide and its toxins had been carried by the air and had caused my roses to wilt.

Not long afterwards I went to the Royal Agricultural Show in Coventry and came across this little tent run by an organic farmer. I spent two hours with him and he explained to me what being organic meant and how we could raise our animals and grow our crops in a sustainable and natural way without pesticides or antibiotics. On the way home I recall saying to my husband, 'We can't carry on farming the way we are; we have to do it differently.'

I went to our farm manager who showered me with arguments about how we wouldn't be as productive and that profit would go down, but he agreed to try it on 30 acres. It took three years to get them up and going, and seven for the whole farm to become organic. And I remember our wonderful shepherd Dick coming to me and saying, 'Do you know, you were so right – the animals are happier; they're healthier because we're treating them homeopathically, and the lamb has a better flavour.'

Organic farming isn't the easy path – crops fail, the weather interferes with your plans and you have to pick yourself up from the ashes sometimes – but I've never looked back.

Holistic living

When we started to farm in this way I often came up against resistance. People couldn't understand why we wanted to do it, and I was battling against fixed notions of what being organic meant and whether organic food really was better for you. But it feels as though we're currently at a turning point. There's a wider awareness and acceptance that what goes into our body is so important for our overall health and well-being; and people are understanding that we do need to live in a holistic way – to look after our body, mind and spirit – not just because it makes sense for us but because it makes sense for the world and for the long-term health of our planet.

For me eating organically is a chain; it starts with healthy soil and ends with nutritious food and a healthier planet.

In a way we've come full circle. More and more people want to know what they're eating and how their food is produced, and they're asking more questions. Organic food is more expensive. It has to be. There was a time when eating organically was considered an extravagant luxury, but attitudes are changing. People are shopping more consciously, and instead of going around a supermarket and buying far too much and wasting it, they are buying what they know they need and finding out where their food is from and how it was produced; they're moving away from supermarkets towards supporting local shops and smaller, artisan producers and businesses who are mindful of their ethical and environmental footprint.

I do eat things that aren't organic – it's not possible to eat organically all of the time, especially if you travel. Life is for living and you'd miss out on all kinds of experiences if you were militant about always eating organic produce. I do eat the occasional avocado – we can't grow them successfully in this country – but 80 per cent of what I eat is organic, and above all it's local and it's seasonal. And if an ingredient has travelled far then I think about it; that choice is considered.

I don't follow any kind of food philosophy. Eating well is about flavour and nutrition and balance. I eat in sync with the seasons in a way that's balanced for my body and mindful for our planet; and as far as is possible that means eating organically and locally, healthily and happily. Yes I have a cold-pressed juice most mornings, but I also love a wonderful cheeseboard and that can be as nourishing for my soul as any green juice can be for my body. I am not going to fixate on eating something organic if it doesn't taste as good as food that's been grown locally, or farmed with care and intelligence. The only thing I truly avoid is processed food.

This book features recipes for different times of the day and for different occasions, whether you're eating alone, preparing food for family and friends, or eating outdoors, which I adore. The recipes are organised by season. I like my food to really taste of its ingredients, which means it has to be simple, fresh and designed to celebrate produce rather than be flashy or fussy. There are, however, a few dishes in the book that are a little bit more complex. I love entertaining and a dinner party is a time when I do want to impress, so these recipes are for times when you want to push the boat out a little. There is also a section at the end with a particular focus on well-being – recipes for days when you're feeling like you need a boost or want to nurture your body with extra vitamins and goodness.

At Daylesford we grow, farm and produce in harmony with nature.

You will find several recipes that encourage reducing or preventing food waste; designed to enable you to preserve produce, use up your leftovers or cook the lesser used, often discarded, parts of an animal, such as offal. Waste, and the resulting greenhouse gases it creates, has become one of the greatest threats to the health of our planet and atmosphere and the statistics outlining how much food and packaging we discard each year are frightening. It is something I am committed to tackling as much as we can, so buying, eating and packaging in a mindful way is one of our key sustainability principles at Daylesford. None of our London food waste is sent to landfill and our unsold fresh food is sent to charities and local soup kitchens (see page 254). At the farm, all our scraps from the café and production kitchen are a valuable source of goodness for our compost heap, which in turn is used to nourish our market garden. Our packaging is also a primary concern. Of course there are always improvements to be made, but we do our best to package as lightly as we can, using natural materials that can be reused, recycled or composted. Since we opened the farm shops we have had 'bags for life' and have never had a plastic carrier bag anywhere at Daylesford.

Our milk packaging is something I am particularly proud of. The innovative pouch that our creamery uses is made from Calymer, which contains 40 per cent chalk, a natural material that requires no chemical processes to extract it and uses minimal energy to produce. The packaging's carbon footprint is significantly lower when compared to a standard HDPE plastic bottle.

Living from the land

Nature is of course the beating heart, the life and soul of everything we do on a farm. But beyond the fields, remaining connected to the earth; nurturing and working in tandem with its bounty is fundamental to everything I do and believe in. I feel an almost acute need to be in nature. For me it is our richest source of beauty and that is why I'm so passionate about the work we do at Daylesford to care for it. There's a poem by Keats titled 'A Thing of Beauty is a Joy Forever' and those words have always resonated with me because I want us all to be able to surround ourselves with beauty whenever we can. Nature is God's gift to us and it's up to us to look after it, to ensure that future generations can enjoy its miracles too.

People often ask me how I find the energy and it's simply because I love life. I'm permanently curious. I always think I'm going to go round the next corner and find a treasure and I believe there's forever something more to learn. Life is a feast, and it's up to us to enjoy every minute of it.

CONSCIOUS LIVING

Daylesford was born out of a desire to make a difference, and the core principles on which it was founded continue to govern my decisions and drive my ideas. Above all these principles are at the heart of all the work that my team and I do at the farm and through my other endeavours. Below are some of the beliefs and principles I strive to follow as best I can, and as far as is possible, in order to lead a more conscious way of life. My hope is that they will inspire you to adopt some of them too.

Nurture nature; don't fight it

Look after the long-term health of our planet by working in harmony with the environment

Farm sustainably and responsibly — farm organically

Shop and eat locally and seasonally

Be mindful of our ethical and environmental footprint; reuse, recycle and package lightly

Nourish body, mind and spirit

Pass on knowledge: teach and inspire the next generation

Safeguard artisan traditions, skills and values

Give back

Being in nature, surrounding myself with wild green beauty, calms my mind and nurtures my soul.

THE CREAMERY

At the farm the day begins at around 5am when our herdsman leads our cows into the parlour for milking. We founded Daylesford with a small herd of dairy cows and today our pedigree British Friesian and rare-breed Gloucester herds and the organic milk they each provide are still at the heart of what we do.

Just a few steps from the milking parlour is the farm's busy creamery. The fresh milk is pumped directly from the parlour into our milk house and cheese room.

Everything we produce at the creamery is designed to ensure that none of our milk is wasted. In the milk house, most of the milk is packaged up to be sold in our sustainable pouches. We skim the cream from certain batches of milk to make skimmed and semi-skimmed milk, but instead of being thrown away, the cream is churned and rolled by hand to produce our pats of butter. The by-product of that churning – the buttermilk – is also collected and sold in our farm shops. I'm particularly fond of it in scones; it gives them a wonderfully light texture.

Live cultures are added to one batch of milk to create thick, creamy yoghurt, while in a separate vat, the milk is mixed with live yeasts to produce our fermented milk drink, kefir. The natural ferments are easier to digest and kefir is believed to help restore the natural balance of healthy flora in our guts.

In the cheese room our small team develops, matures and moulds nine different cheeses, from blues and goat's cheese to Single and Double Gloucesters, Cheddar and another hard cheese named after the local village of Adlestrop. We continue to honour traditional methods of cheesemaking, separating the curds from the whey by hand, using wooden pulley systems to weight and press the cheeses, and relying on intuition and skill to judge when the cheeses have ripened to be at their best.

The nature of organic milk means that it will change throughout the year, according to the weather, the season and the behaviour of the herd, so our cheesemakers must understand and work in harmony with its natural properties and their mutations. Rather than standardising processes and flavours, we adjust our recipes to the milk and believe that it is this artisan, small-scale production that gives our cheeses their distinctive flavours.

The cooked cheese curds used to produce our hard cheeses are poured into moulds then pressed slowly and gently, and the cheeses are turned by hand. Pressing too quickly means that our cheesemakers might find liquid – essentially butter – stuck to the bottom of the moulds so they must check each cheese regularly to ensure it is being pressed at the right speed. Nothing is rushed. Our Single Gloucester cheese matures for eight weeks, while our Cheddar will be aged for anything up to 18 months. We monitor every stage of the process closely – even the muslin cloths we use to wrap our cheeses are made from organic cotton.

Our expert team relies on intuition, skill and senses, but above all they have a deep understanding of the natural make-up of their ingredient, in order to nurture its very best qualities.

OUR GLOUCESTER HERD

Gloucestershire has a long history of making cheese, and for many years the Single Gloucester was one of the most common in the county, a household staple made from the milk of the local Old Gloucester cattle.

In the mid-eighteenth century a cattle plague depleted stocks of Old Gloucester cattle to the point where it became a rare breed, and this, along with falling demand meant production virtually ceased. Eventually the cattle became so scarce that in 1994 Single Gloucester cheese was granted Protected Designation of Origin (PDO) status.

After rescuing and breeding a herd of pure Old Gloucester cattle, we are now one of only six producers in the UK to be allowed to make the cheese. To guarantee the purest, most authentic flavour, we choose only to use milk from our Single Gloucester herd and we milk them separately from our Friesians. The cheese's mild, buttery flavour relies heavily on the quality of the milk; there's nothing in the production process that can hide any faults.

Single Gloucester was obsolete for such a long time that for me and for our cheesemakers it's not only a privilege to have been part of its renaissance, it's rewarding to think we're part of a small group trying to reinvent it; writing a new chapter in its history. It also just happens to be my favourite.

A cheese for all seasons

I cannot resist a cheeseboard. I love the depth of flavour that comes from a good cheese and while I definitely have my favourites, I'm always keen to learn about and try new types and experiment with the kinds of cheeses I serve. As with all seasonal produce, there are times of the year when certain ones will be at their best but I don't believe cheese should be something to cause confusion; it is there to be enjoyed. When making up a board I generally just choose a hard cheese, a sheep or a goat's cheese, a blue, a soft cheese and then a cheese that is particular to that season, like a Mont d'Or in winter or Wigmore in the summer.

In terms of what to pair with them, you're never going to find something that marries with all of the different flavours so just pick a single cheese and serve accompaniments that work well with it.

Opposite is a brief guide to what you can expect if you choose some of our cheeses; though of course, choosing cheeses that are local to you will inevitably enrich your enjoyment of one of life's greatest joys.

1. Daylesford Cheddar
I'll often have our Cheddar on a cheeseboard throughout the year as it's always popular thanks to its familiar flavour – but for me Cheddar is a must at Christmastime. By then ours will have been aged for up to 18 months meaning it is deeply-flavoured, rich and mature.

2. Daylesford Blue
Our Daylesford Blue is a firm blue with a buttery texture and with a sharpness that is not overpowering.

3. Artemis Greek-Style
A salty, crumbly cheese, very much like a Greek feta cheese; it's wonderful in salads.

4. Bledington Blue
Bledington Blue is our soft, creamy blue which has an almost spicy flavour. It's creamy and milder than something like a Stilton so even people who think they don't like blue cheeses often enjoy this one.

5. Foscot
Foscot is our mild, very soft cheese; a couple are flavoured, either with truffle or sage and honey.

6. Baywell
Baywell is a soft, nearly runny cow's cheese which has a strong, almost herb-like flavour.

7. Single Gloucester
Single Gloucester is a delicate and mild-flavoured hard cheese, very different to Double Gloucester – it's my absolute favourite.

8. Double Gloucester
Our Double Gloucester has a particularly nutty yet mellow flavour.

9. Adlestrop
Adlestrop is our semi-soft cheese. Underneath the thick rind is a mild and buttery cheese with a slightly crumbly texture.

THE BAKERY

Baking good bread takes time. It's a simple fact, yet it's a philosophy that has for the large part been lost at some point in Britain's bread-making history. At the farm, our bakery team has taken baking back to its origins. We make our bread following artisanal, hand-led methods, using no more than the basic ingredients loaves have been baked with for centuries: flour, water and salt.

Our bakers rely on traditional bread-making methods, kneading and shaping their doughs by hand, then leaving them to prove, rise and develop flavour according to their natural timescale.

We source the highest quality organic flours and natural ingredients to bake breads, cakes and pastries that reflect the philosophy at the heart of the way we cook and eat.

While commercial bakeries rely on a processed 'fast-action' yeast to shorten a dough's leavening process, then pump their goods full of preservatives and additives to inject flavour and improve shelf life, we bake our breads using a natural leaven – a sourdough culture or 'starter' – made from a simple mixture of flour and water and natural bacteria from the surrounding environment.

Our loaves slowly ferment for at least 10 hours, allowing the dough the time it needs to develop the bread's elasticity and texture.

It is this nurturing, this respect for an ingredient's natural properties, that gives our breads their depth of flavour and our sourdough loaves their distinctive chewiness and tang.

Beyond the better flavour, embracing this slowness has also been proven to be kinder to our bodies. During the long fermentation process, important nutrients, such as iron, zinc and magnesium, folic acid and other B vitamins, become easier for our bodies to absorb. For us, this is one of the reminders that a slower, simpler way of living and respecting the produce we are lucky enough to enjoy is not just about keeping traditions alive; it's about ensuring a healthy future.

MAKES 2 LOAVES

Potato and thyme sourdough

Making a sourdough loaf at home does require more time and patience than a standard loaf, but you'll be rewarded in terms of its more complex flavour, its wonderful chewy texture and in the benefits it brings to your body (see page 34). This hearty, herby offering is perfect comfort food in the autumn and winter months; I think it makes wonderful cheese on toast, served with a little mustard on the side for a hint of heat.

500g waxy potatoes such as Desiree, peeled
2 tbsp olive oil
500g strong white bread flour, plus extra for dusting
400g sourdough starter (see below)

1½ tbsp olive oil
280ml lukewarm water
2 level tbsp chopped thyme leaves
1 level tsp salt

Preheat the oven to 180°C/gas 4. Cut the potatoes in half and place in a baking tray. Toss with the oil and roast for about 50 minutes, making sure they don't burn. Remove from the tray and cool, then cut into chunks.

Put all the ingredients, except for the salt and potatoes, in a sturdy kitchen mixer fitted with the hook attachment. Mix on slow speed for 4 minutes, then on high speed for a further 5 minutes. Add the salt and mix again on fast speed for a final 8 minutes. Transfer to a floured bowl, cover with a damp tea towel and leave to rise in a warm place for a few hours. Depending on the conditions, this can take between 1 and 4 hours. The dough should be risen and doubled in size.

Turn the dough out onto a lightly floured surface and knead in the potato cubes so they are as evenly distributed as possible. Divide the dough into two even pieces and place in floured bannetons (proving baskets). Dust the bread liberally with flour and leave to rise again in a warm place until doubled in size, about 8 hours (you can do this overnight). If you don't have bannetons, place the dough on a lined baking tray and shape into a country loaf before leaving to rise.

Preheat the oven to 220°C/gas 7. Transfer the risen loaves to a lined baking tray (if in bannetons), dust with flour and bake for about 25 minutes until a golden crust has formed. If you like, you can try adding a handful of ice cubes into the bottom of the oven before baking your bread. This creates steam, which in turn produces a better crust. Remove from the oven and transfer to a wire rack to cool.

SOURDOUGH STARTER

75g strong white bread flour
75ml lukewarm water

You'll need to start this at least a week before you need it. Mix together the flour and water in a large warm sterilised jar (see page 201). Stir together well and leave at room temperature, uncovered. For the next 3 days remove a little of the starter and discard and then replace that amount with the same amount of flour and water and stir.

After 3 days it should be beginning to bubble and smell of fermentation. Cover the jar loosely with a tea towel. The starter should be very bubbly and ready to use after 6 days; if not, carry on feeding with the flour and water. When you remove some of the starter to use for baking, top it back up with 125g flour and 25ml lukewarm water and keep the jar loosely covered. If you are not baking for a while, leave the starter in the fridge, but uncover and bring to room temperature before using in order to activate it.

MAKES 2 LOAVES

Honey, fig and walnut sourdough

Each season our bakery team creates a new loaf for the farm shops that celebrates some of the best of that season's produce. This is one I'm particularly fond of. In September, our farm honey will just have been harvested. It lends the bread a gentle sweetness, which contrasts with the tang of the mildly sour dough; and the first wet walnuts — one of my favourite autumnal treasures — will just have appeared. Freshly baked or toasted, all this bread needs is a good lick of creamy organic butter.

305g strong white bread flour
305g malted bread flour
245g Sourdough Starter (see page 38)
385ml water, at room temperature
2 tbsp clear honey
2 tsp salt
150g dried figs, chopped
75g walnuts, chopped
rice flour, for dusting

Before starting this recipe you will need to have prepared the sourdough starter following the recipe on page 38.

Place the flours, starter, water and honey in a kitchen mixer. Using the hook attachment, mix on slow speed for 4 minutes and then on high speed for 4 more minutes. Add the salt, figs and walnuts and mix on high speed for another 4 more minutes. Transfer to a floured bowl, cover with a damp tea towel and leave to rise in a warm place for about 6 hours.

Divide the dough into two equal pieces. Shape into nice round balls and place on a baking tray, dusted with rice flour. Leave to prove overnight in a warm place until doubled in size.

Preheat the oven to 220°C/gas 7. Transfer the risen loaves to a lined baking tray (if in bannetons), dust with rice flour again and bake for about 25 minutes until a golden crust has formed. If you like, you can try adding a handful of ice cubes into the bottom of the oven before baking your bread. This creates steam, which in turn produces a better crust. Remove from the oven and transfer to a wire rack to cool.

OUR ANIMALS

The welfare of our animals has and always will be our biggest priority at Daylesford and this stems right from the farm's beginnings when we chose the breeds we were going to rear. From our British Friesians, Gloucester cattle and Legbar hens to our flocks of Ryeland and Kerry Hill sheep, raising our animals in the most caring way is at the heart of our farming philosophy.

Above: our Lleyn sheep; left: our herd of deer at Wootton

In the early days of the organic movement in the UK, many who believed in and focused on an industrial, intensive style of agriculture thought that we were mad to try and make the switch to organic. But one of the reasons I am so proud of the work we do is because I know you can see its benefits in the health and vitality of our animals. When our Senior farms manager Richard Smith drives visitors around our fields, the sleek coats and bright eyes of our livestock are enough to silence even the most ardent sceptics.

Not only can you see the health and vitality in our animals, you can experience the benefits to your own health and judge the improved taste in our meat. Animals raised on a nutrient-rich pasture diet produce meat that is much higher in essential omega fatty acids, as well as vitamins A and E, and it is free from additives.

To farm organically is to farm without the use of pesticides, artificial fertilisers, antibiotics or any other chemicals. But beyond this, for me organic farming is about slowing things down. It is about returning to traditional means of producing food, in harmony with our environment and with nature. And it is about ensuring this food production is sustainable – that the generations to follow will continue to enjoy the resources we do. One of the questions I get asked most often is whether organic farming can feed the world. The short answer is that it can. It did so for hundreds of generations – we're only two or three on from a time when organic farming was the only form of farming. There is a belief that the slowness, the seeming luxury of affording animals space to roam and rotating crops to ensure good soil health is the talk of a few dreamers and not practical to feed the world's soaring population. I don't believe that. You need to understand the principles behind organic agriculture and how to manage it – with knowledge and expertise it can, and I hope will, one day feed the world.

CATTLE

Aside from our dairy herd of British Friesians, we raise beef cattle: South Devon cows at Daylesford and Aberdeen Angus up at Wootton. Both are raised in their natural environments in habitats that reflect the origins of each breed. I also wanted to add a rare breed of cattle to the farm. Supporting rare breeds is something I am very passionate about – we're in danger of losing so many of our native breeds simply because they're not popular or not deemed productive enough, but losing our heritage would be a futile tragedy and I believe that we have a duty and a responsibility to ensure that these breeds don't die out.

It was a wet Saturday in August when Richard went off to a sale that was advertised as selling Gloucesteshire-farmed animals. We'd talked about him looking out for a breed called White Parks, but when he arrived at the sale yard, there was a handful of Gloucester cattle, one of Britain's oldest and rarest native breeds. Given our home in Kingham, the breed seemed like a natural fit for Daylesford. I remember the day Richard brought them back to the farm – they were gentle and quiet and very beautiful with their dark, almost chocolate-coloured coats.

We went on to add to the cows Richard managed to buy at that sale, to create a small herd. In 1972 there were only 52 registered Gloucester cows left in the world; today we have 70 on our farm and a handful of bulls, and Richard, his farm team and I are all extremely proud of the work that has gone into their conservation and survival.

Above: our rare-breed Gloucester cattle; left: one of our Aberdeen Angus bulls; overleaf: the striking black markings of our pedigree Kerry Hill sheep never fail to bring a smile

HENS AND EGGS

Among the brambles up on Wootton's parkland were three chicken houses that my father-in-law had inherited from the house's previous owners. They hadn't been used in years so when I decided that the farm shop should be stocking our own eggs, we brought the houses down to Daylesford, cleaned them and put them in the field for our newly-acquired flock of organic hens.

Unlike larger animals, hens have simple needs. If they have access to plenty of sunlight and space and are free of stress, hens will lay. Our hens produce rich organic eggs with bright golden yolks and a delicious flavour. A few years after the first hens arrived at the farm, we added to our flock when a local farmer sold us his Legbar hens. A traditional British breed, Legbars are famous for their beautiful pastel-blue eggshells, which range from a creamy, very pale colour to a light green. Legbar hens are a minority breed in the UK so again, I'm very proud to be supporting their survival.

At Wootton, we also rear chickens for the table. One of the challenges facing so many farmers today is that chickens are at risk of developing health problems. Newborn chicks are very fragile and vulnerable at birth and the first 24 hours of their lives are very important in determining whether they will go on to have a healthy future. At our hatchery our team is able to monitor our chicks' births carefully to guarantee the safest conditions and allow them to grow into happy chickens producing the very best quality of meat.

Right: our egg-laying Legbar hens

THE MARKET GARDEN

Like many things at Daylesford, our market garden has grown quite instinctively and naturally, almost by chance. In the first year, when we were really concentrating solely on livestock, I would sometimes bring over cuttings of fruit or vegetables I had gluts of in my own garden and plant them in the vegetable patch at the farm. And as things took and we were able to sell a small amount of fruit and vegetables, we started to plan a more comprehensive plot.

We try to grow things that you can't always buy in supermarkets – interesting, more unusual varieties that customers will enjoy experimenting with, perhaps discovering new flavours or textures. And although our head gardener Jez will always have one eye on the farm shop and what people will expect and want to find there, the other is intently focused on planning the garden to ensure we have enough to see us through the year, and on what we can grow. In reality, so much of growing, particularly in an organic system, depends on your soil. Growing is about understanding the local soil conditions and sowing what is going to succeed, then rotating the crops in order to maintain soil health and ensure you will be able to grow again the following year.

The market garden has become the heart of the farm, governing so much of what else goes on here. It drives the menus at the cafés: our chefs change and devise them according to the produce that is available in the garden, and for the cookery school it's the first port of call in showing visitors where the ingredients they are cooking with come from. But aside from the joy it brings to our plates, above all, for me, the garden is so integral to the work we do as a way of demonstrating why we believe eating seasonally is so important.

We live in a world where we have access to most types of produce all the year round, yet both my team and I fervently believe that eating food that has been grown locally to you, in harmony with nature's natural cycles, is the right way to eat. Nutritionally it is better for our bodies; it is helping us to protect and secure

the long-term health of our planet; and I believe it is infinitely better in flavour. For how can a tomato bought in January – an insipid, watery fruit that has travelled or been forced to grow without sunlight – taste as fresh or as vibrant as a pea that's been picked on a warm sunny spring day? Even putting aside the environmental and sustainability arguments, food that grows according to its seasonal climate and has not had to sustain months of storage and travel simply tastes better.

INSPIRED BY INGREDIENTS

I'm often asked what inspires me and how I get my ideas, and the shortest answer is 'ingredients'. I crave contact with ingredients and raw materials – from the fruit and vegetables we grow in the market garden to the logs around the woodland and farm. I love touching and seeing produce in its purest form. So it follows that one of my greatest sources of inspiration (and joy) comes from visiting markets – food, craft and antiques markets. The first thing I'll do when I go to a new country or place is go to the local food market in the very early morning. I love watching all the goings-on at that time – familiarising myself with the sights, sounds and smells. You can start to get a feel for a culture through the interactions of the vendors with their customers, or just a sense of the flavours, styles and foods. Markets tug at all my senses, stimulating thought and creativity and it's inevitably after a visit to a market abroad that I am struck by a new idea. There's a lot to learn and a rummage among the stalls never fails to inspire me to think about small changes we could make at Daylesford, whether it's a new variety of tomato to try growing or a style of ceramic we could bring to the cafés.

WORKING WITH CHEFS

I love being in the kitchen. I am not a natural cook but I absolutely love spending time with chefs and watching them work; I admire them. Chefs are artisans: they have amazing skill but they also have a passion and an enthusiasm for what they do that I find infectious.

I work very closely with chefs, particularly the chefs who create the menus in our cafés and restaurants. We discuss ideas and recipes and how to make the most of what's currently in season, but I've also worked with chefs who have come to the farm to learn about produce. Some chefs that work in urban environments can be very removed from the source of their work. They are used to picking up a telephone to track down their ingredients and coming to the farm can be quite an eye-opening experience for them. It's wonderful to see them learn about choosing their produce and enjoying the proximity to nature – to the farm and garden. I hope that in a tiny way I may have helped nurture a deeper interest in their ingredients and where they come from – the roots and heart of their craft. And in turn I've learned so much about flavours, pairings and dishes from them.

THE FARM SHOPS

The year that we produced our first cheese, we also set up a little bakery to bake sourdough loaves, and the idea for a farm shop simply grew from there. I was looking at one of the empty barns and said to my husband, 'Do you think I could open a farm shop?'

We opened three weeks before Christmas on a frosty morning, selling homemade soups, sandwiches and tea, alongside our meat, cheese, a few vegetables and our bread. I didn't think anybody would come. I was terrified; how would they even know it was there? At the time the farm was really just a few fields in the middle of nowhere so I couldn't imagine anybody stumbling across our shop. I think that it was only because it was Christmas and we were selling organic turkeys that a few passers-by spotted the sign at the end of the track and came in to see what we were doing and whether they could buy their Christmas bird.

When I look back I really loved the first two or three years of the shop. We were so tiny and you got to know everybody so well – we knew the regulars' names and all the locals from the village. The first day I was there until 2am stacking shelves and getting things ready but I remember loving the anticipation and excitement of it all.

And the journey hasn't been easy. Like any business, we've had our setbacks and challenges. One year we had a terrible fire so we had to set up trestle tables outside, but despite that we've managed to grow, and we now have five shops (four in London). Each has its own personality while remaining very true to the style and philosophy of the original.

I love the traditional side of a farm shop, and for me that's about having the best jams and marmalades alongside great bread, fresh milk and eggs and vegetables;

but I also love the innovative aspect to it, the opportunity to move with trends and reflect changing tastes and demands in what people are eating. And I suppose because I'm older now, I like seeing how things go full circle and come back into fashion – whether it's bone broths, dumplings or a resurgence in the cheaper cuts of meat I ate as a child. Retail and its rhythms never cease to fascinate me. When I opened the farm shop, it was at a time when 'organic' was still considered

BLACKBERRIES MEDLAR ROSEHIPS   WINTER BRUSSELS SPROUTS PARSNIPS

Our log slice walls and panels have become a recurring feature of the architecture at Daylesford. I like using wood for the warmth and tactility it brings to an interior but it also enables us to recycle one of nature's gifts and most precious resources. The logs used to make the heart above came from holly trees that fell naturally at the farm

a little bit rustic – a bit alternative and possibly a bit hippy and 'out there', so in some ways I had a clean slate when I designed the shop. I just followed my instincts and went with what I liked, and I suppose in a sense I changed the general notion of how a farm shop could or should look without even really realising it.

I was lucky enough to have met an architect – Spencer Fung – very early on. It was his wife Teresa, who introduced us and I knew I'd found a kindred spirit. Spencer thinks just like I do. He shares my love of nature and of recycling materials and he believes in the importance of sustainability, so he was very good at understanding me and my vision

The farm shops are all set within old buildings – be that a farmyard barn or an eighteenth-century London townhouse –

and I like to appreciate and respect the features of the old buildings, but also bring something new and modern to them. It means you might find a white concrete floor set against the bare brickwork of a Cotswold stone barn. I love the contrast of the old and the new. And if I'm looking at a building I'll always take it back. If something's got wallpaper I always want to pull it off and see what the bricks look like; or rip up the floors to see what's underneath.

The colours and materials I use are definitely inspired by nature. We use a lot of wood – recycled where we can – and other strong, hard-wearing natural materials such as stone and marble. And as much as possible the materials are sourced from our surrounding area and the work is carried out by hand, by local craftsmen.

I like to celebrate the original structure and features of an agricultural building – its brickwork, wooden beams and masonry; revealing the building's history but using its bones to create a contemporary, modern space.

THE OLD SPOT

I've always wanted everybody who comes to the farm to be able to enjoy their visit in a way that suits them and their mood. There's plenty for children and families but it was important to me to have a space that felt more grown-up.

I wanted somewhere I could indulge my own love of a good cocktail and eat the kind of food that comes with afternoons in the sunshine when you don't necessarily want a heavy meal, but to graze on simple things as you sip a cold drink.

Named after the Gloucester pig, the Old Spot bar is one of the places I love most at the farm. Tucked behind the farm shop, it's an open, high-ceilinged room, flooded with natural light. It comes into its own on sunny days and balmy evenings where you can come and enjoy a foraged botanical cocktail, a glass of wine or a quiet morning coffee at the bar and spill out on to the courtyard garden tables outside. In the winter, a charcoal oven and rotisserie keep the bar warm and welcoming; while wood-fired pizzas topped with seasonal ingredients from the garden provide comfort food to nourish the soul and hearty stews nurture the body. Whether I'm pulling up a stool at the Old Spot bar on my own, or gathering friends to savour a cocktail, I know it's somewhere I can kick back and have a bit of fun.

EACH MAKES 2 PIZZAS

TRADITIONAL PIZZA DOUGH

250g Italian tipo '00' flour or strong bread flour
3g fast-action dried yeast
175ml water
1½ tbsp olive oil
1 level tsp salt

SPELT PIZZA DOUGH

175g white spelt flour
75g wholemeal spelt flour
4g fast-action dried yeast
150ml lukewarm water
1½ tbsp olive oil
1 level tsp salt

Mix the flour(s) and yeast together in a large bowl or kitchen mixer fitted with a hook attachment. Gradually add the water and olive oil until it comes together. Leave for 5 minutes then add the salt and knead lightly for 1 minute. Leave for another 5 minutes and then carry on kneading lightly. Shape into a ball, cover with a damp cloth and leave to prove for about an hour until it is 1½ times its original size. Divide the dough into two and shape into neat, tight balls. Cover and rest for 15 minutes.

EACH MAKES 2 PIZZAS

Single Gloucester pizza

1 quantity pizza dough (see page 72)
flour and semolina, for dusting
250g heritage tomatoes, sliced
100g Single Gloucester cheese, grated
olive oil, for drizzling

FOR THE TOMATO SAUCE
2 tbsp olive oil
1 onion, sliced
2 garlic cloves, crushed
1 x 400g tin chopped tomatoes
20g basil leaves, plus a few extra to garnish
salt and pepper

For the tomato sauce, heat the olive oil in a pan, add the onion and cook gently until soft. Add the garlic and when it turns golden, add the tomatoes and reduce the heat. Season to taste and simmer for 30–40 minutes, adding a splash of water if it gets too dry. Add the basil and leave to infuse off the heat for about 30 minutes. Blitz lightly using a hand-held blender.

Preheat the oven to 200°C/gas 6. Put two large baking sheets into the oven to heat. Roll each dough ball out on a surface lightly dusted with a little flour and semolina and shape into rough rounds.

Spread half the tomato sauce over each pizza, leaving a border around the edge. Cover each with half the tomatoes and cheese. Drizzle with a little oil and slide the pizzas on to the hot baking sheets. Bake for 15–20 minutes until golden brown. Serve scattered with a few basil leaves.

Sprouting broccoli pizza

1 quantity pizza dough (see page 72)
spelt flour, for dusting
300ml crème fraîche
220g tenderstem broccoli, blanched for 3 minutes and refreshed in cold water
1 red chilli, deseeded and chopped
4 tbsp pesto (see below)
olive oil, for drizzling

FOR THE PESTO
2 garlic cloves, crushed
50g parsley, roughly chopped
30g blanched hazelnuts, chopped
150ml olive oil
55g Cheddar, grated
salt and pepper

For the pesto, put the garlic and parsley into a food processor, add the chopped nuts and pulse to combine. With the engine running, slowly pour in the oil. Add the cheese, then season to taste. Any left over will keep in an airtight jar in the fridge for a week and is delicious with pasta or new potatoes.

Preheat the oven and roll out the dough as above. Spread half the crème fraîche on each pizza, leaving a clear border around the edge. Cut the thicker broccoli stems in half lengthways and put half on each pizza, along with half the chilli. Spoon 2 tablespoons of pesto over each pizza. Finish and bake the pizzas as above.

BOTANICAL MOCKTAILS • EACH SERVES 1

The mocktails and cocktails we serve at the Old Spot all draw inspiration from the garden. Fresh, zesty, invigorating, vibrant and even cleansing – there's something for everyone.

Vitamin tonic

50ml pink grapefruit juice
20ml lemon juice
30ml honey syrup
1cm thick slice of fresh ginger
soda water, to top up
dehydrated lemon slice or fresh
    lemon twist, to garnish

FOR THE HONEY SYRUP
50ml clear honey
50ml water

First make the syrup: mix the honey and water, pour into a clean bottle and store in the fridge – the syrup will keep for up to 2 weeks.

To make the cocktail, add all but the soda water to an ice-filled cocktail shaker. Shake and strain into a champagne flute and top up with soda water. Garnish with your choice.

Orchard punch

75ml apple juice
75ml pomegranate juice
15ml elderflower cordial
15ml lemon juice
crushed ice, to serve
apple slice and edible flower,
    to garnish (optional)

Add all the ingredients to a cocktail shaker with a handful of ice cubes. Shake vigorously to combine.

Strain into an ice-filled rocks glass and garnish with a slice of apple and an edible flower, if using.

BOTANICAL COCKTAILS • EACH SERVES 1

English garden

1cm slice cucumber
8–10 mint leaves, plus a sprig to garnish
50ml gin
25ml elderflower cordial
25ml lemon juice
crushed ice
apple slice and edible flower, to garnish (optional)

Quarter the slice of cucumber and put the chunks into a tumbler. Muddle with a cocktail muddler or the end of a rolling pin or wooden spoon. Rub the mint between your fingers then add it to the glass along with the gin, elderflower cordial and lemon juice. Top up with crushed ice, then stir the bottom with a bar spoon. Top with more ice before garnishing with the apple, mint and edible flower, if using.

Matcha sour

50ml vodka
3 mint leaves
2 cucumber chunks
50ml apple juice
25ml lemon juice
25ml sugar syrup (shop-bought, or make your own using a 2:1 ratio of sugar to water)
1 medium egg white
tiny pinch of matcha powder, to garnish

Put a martini glass in the freezer to chill. Add all the ingredients except the matcha to an ice-filled shaker and shake hard for 10 seconds. Discard the ice then shake again to create a foam. Strain into your chilled martini glass and decorate with a sprinkle of matcha powder.

Pea shoot sour

50ml gin
25ml lemon juice
25ml pea syrup (see below)
1 medium egg white
pea pod or pea shoot, to garnish

FOR THE PEA SYRUP
100ml sugar syrup (shop-bought, or make your own using a 2:1 ratio of sugar to water)
50g garden peas

Blitz the syrup ingredients in a blender until thick and smooth, with as few lumps as possible. Pour into a glass jar or bottle – it will keep in the fridge for up to 5 days. For the cocktail, put all the ingredients into an ice-filled cocktail shaker and shake hard for 10 seconds. Discard the ice then shake again to create a foam. Strain into a chilled Martini or champagne glass and garnish.

THE COOKERY SCHOOL

Setting up a cookery school at the farm was a way of giving visitors the opportunity to share our ingredients – the heart of everything we do at Daylesford – and to reconnect with them; to use and engage with produce while also learning about it and understanding how it journeys from field to fork.

I feel very fortunate to be surrounded by people from whom I am constantly learning. I learn from my children, from my grandchildren and I learn a lot from my team at the farm. Knowledge is something I value enormously, so the idea of sharing and passing on knowledge, particularly to the next generation, is something that is very important to me.

Most of us need to cook every day, but in a world where speed and convenience have become driving priorities, cooking from scratch is something that can get pushed aside – it seems easier to reach for the ready-made tomato sauce instead of making one using fresh ingredients. And even for those who do cook, the path our food takes to end up on our plates is something from which many have become disconnected.

All the courses we offer at the cookery school are based around the principle I firmly believe in: cooking seasonally. Eating well doesn't have to be hard and it shouldn't be complicated: eat seasonally, eat locally and treat your ingredients simply and with respect and not only do you look after your health, you look after your family and you look after our planet.

The courses are about teaching understanding. Our tutors won't just show you how to make an oxtail stew, they'll explain why using cheaper cuts such as oxtail can benefit your health because of its nutrients; why you need to sweat the onions very slowly to create the rich base for the stew; and why using every bit of an animal – boiling the bones to make stocks or using marrow to add flavour, texture and nourishment – is not only important in avoiding food waste, but also in enriching your cooking and ultimately saving you time.

We have cooks arrive with different levels of experience – from complete beginners to those who cook regularly – but all want to learn a new skill or be inspired by the themes of the courses we offer, be that dinner party suppers or how to entertain at Christmas, to fermenting, cooking with seafood or how to make good homemade bread. The school is also a way of passing on skills that are perhaps no longer as familiar to us as they were to previous generations. One of the questions our teachers get asked most often, for example, is how to poach an egg. We've lost some of our fundamental skills and instincts and I wanted to provide a means for people to access those skills again, in a relaxed and inspiring environment, however confident or experienced they are in the kitchen.

Although we grow our own produce at the farm, foraging for wild food is an activity that I am very keen to encourage because it's a free and sustainable resource. As long as it's carried out responsibly and you go with someone who has a trained eye, rummaging among the hedgerows, grassy banks and river shallows can provide a plentiful, sustainable and very seasonal source of food and it's a skill that allows everyone to harvest ingredients from their local surroundings.

Foraging is an age-old skill that I don't want to see die out, so our cookery school runs courses on which visitors are taken out into the surrounding countryside by our foraging expert and environmentalist to discover and learn about the world of wild food. The ingredients to be harvested

will of course change with the seasons but the choice is vast. Throughout the year you can expect to find wild salads and greens, edible flowers, herbs, wild berries and hedgerow fruits, crayfish or game. (For more on foraging berries, see page 215.)

Some of our most popular courses at the school are those aimed at children and teenagers, particularly those needing to learn to cook for themselves before they head to college or university. If we can inspire our children to look beyond the tins of baked beans and cook from scratch to nurture their bodies, I will feel happy that the work we do is achieving its aims.

DAYLESFORD GARDEN

Visiting the garden room at Daylesford is peaceful, heavenly and, above all, a feast of soft colours and fragrance. It is our way of trying to bring a touch of the natural world into the home. As far as possible, the flowers, foliage and materials we stock are gathered from our gardens or foraged from the woodland in the surrounding countryside and we also take cuttings, plants and vegetables from the market garden.

SUMMER BOUQUET

I grow a range of flowers in my garden but when I arrange them in vases I like to keep things very simple, often choosing just a single colour for the stems along with a little greenery and foliage. In summer, I frequently turn to white flowers such as double white peonies (7); white spray roses (8); larkspur (1 and 6) and white and green mint (4); but the garden offers such a bounty that I can't resist mixing them with soft tones and shades of another colour – the blues of cornflowers (3); pale blue scabious (9) and pale lilac sweet peas (5). Alchemilla (2) makes a vibrant green accompaniment.

AUTUMN AND WINTER BOUQUET

The winter is the perfect time to forage for cuttings in hedgerows. I like using winter berries such as blackberries (8) and blue-berried viburnum (6), then mixing these with other elements from our market garden such as rosemary. Myrtle (10) is a wonderfully fragrant branch, and bouquets can look very striking, particularly over the festive season if you mix different shapes. Burgundy is a favourite winter colour and I'll combine a range of burgundy stems: amaryllis (9); ranunculus (7); scabious (1) and anemones (3); then mix in a slightly paler shade with buff-coloured Upper Secret roses (4) and spray roses, such as Lydia or Pepita (11). Trailing jasmine and eucalyptus (2 and 5) also add wonderful scents.

DAYLESFORD COTTAGES

Not long after the farm shop opened, we discovered that many people were travelling quite far to visit us. To enable them to break their journey and make their time at the farm more relaxing, I decided to convert some of the old farm buildings as well as a house in the village into self-catering cottages so that people could come and enjoy a longer stay.

Using natural materials gives buildings and furnishings a sense of place. The colour of a stone can evoke its local environment while a wooden or willow chair is a reminder of the trees around us. I love the sense that natural materials bring me closer to nature, even when I'm inside.

Our cottages have become a popular addition to life at Daylesford. Just a few steps from the farm shop but also from the milking sheds, creamery and our café, they feel to me like a haven at the heart of a busy working farm. For many, a stay here has become not only a chance to enjoy all our produce at its freshest but a refuge: it provides an opportunity to reconnect with nature, retreat from the everyday anxieties and stresses of a bustling urban life, or simply experience some of what goes on at the farm first-hand, and the beauty of the Cotswolds countryside.

My aim with the cottages was that they be homes. Homes where visitors could curl up under a cashmere blanket in front of a roaring log fire; share long breakfasts of fresh eggs and organic bacon over the newspapers; or sip a glass of wine while a home-cooked supper simmers on the stove.

Travelling and holidays are a time to indulge, so guests can also enjoy the little luxuries that come with time away from home: beautiful soft linens and bathrobes, fresh cotton sheets, and natural, botanical bath products to nurture their bodies as much as their minds.

The fridges are stocked with milk, a freshly baked loaf sits on the side for toast in the morning, and pantry staples are all within an arm's reach. The cottages are also equipped with all the necessities that life on a working farm commands: racks for muddy wellingtons, logs to stoke the fire and board games for evenings when it's simply that bit too wintry to venture outside.

ANTIQUES

I love the sense of recycling and reuse that comes from buying an antique as well as the chance to give something a new life. Antiquing has long been a passion of mine and I find it hugely satisfying going to seek out unique pieces as well as speaking to the dealers, who are always so generous with their time and knowledge.

At the farm, we've recently launched a room devoted to selling antiques – hand-picked pieces that my team and I source from local antique dealers, markets and fairs. Many of the dealers close to the farm sell practical equipment and agricultural antiques and, while these might not at first sound like obvious places to hunt for furniture, it's amazing what practical objects can be used for if you think a little creatively. I often try to find new uses for pieces collected at these fairs: old laundry tables can be reused as dining tables, sculptors' stands can stand in for stools, and old chopping boards can be hung on walls as decoration; they sit beautifully on the honey-coloured Cotswold stone.

BAMFORD

After we'd made the decision to farm organically, my interest and concern for the way I was doing things grew and I began to look at other areas of my life and question the choices I was making. When I began learning about cotton, I was shocked by some of what went on in order to produce it – what that was doing to the farmers and the environment – and I knew I had to change.

Too many farmers growing cotton non-organically in third-world countries don't wear protective clothing and breathing apparatus; they're inhaling fumes from the chemicals used to process the cotton seeds and as a result they're dying every day. I knew I couldn't go on wearing garments that were responsible for this kind of a death penalty.

It was never my intention to start a fashion label; I simply wanted to create garments that I could feel happy wearing, where I could own and account for each part of the manufacturing process to ensure that the making of the garments embraced the transparency and the ethical principles and philosophy for which the farm stood.

The Bamford clothing range is driven by that desire, from the quality of the yarns and other materials we use and where they are sourced, to who is making the clothing and how. But the range is also very much led by the fabrics themselves and how soft the beautiful natural fibres feel against your skin. I want the clothes to make women feel nurtured by what they put on their bodies, to feel that they are looking after themselves.

We are not a seasonal fashion label; the attention to detail that goes into making these pieces means that they transcend times of year. These are timeless, well-made, beautiful clothes that will last a lifetime, and I hope they will be treasured.

The line also reflects my love of craftsmanship and a strong desire to preserve an industry and skills that we are in danger of losing, not just in the UK but around the world. At the heart of Bamford is the relationships we develop with our suppliers and producers. The workshops and manufacturers are small. They are predominantly family-owned, but above all, they share a legacy and a tradition in textile-making that goes back several generations. They learned their skills from their parents and grandparents and if we don't strive to preserve this precious knowledge, the next generation may never have the chance to harness it.

The pieces at Bamford also embrace a philosophy that drives so much of what I do: the Japanese culture of 'wabi-sabi', a celebration of the beauty of imperfection. I have long been an admirer of Japan, fascinated by its culture, and wabi-sabi is a simple reflection of that admiration, both on the farm and also at Bamford. Being organic is very wabi-sabi – the taste of funny-looking, imperfect apples is incomparable to those that have been picked, preserved and waxed until they're very shiny and have no flavour at all. In the same way, the fabrics we use at Bamford won't always be uniform – there may be a tiny knot in the weave or an imperfection in the yarn, but this is because an artisan has stamped that pattern or woven the loom by hand. You'll see the emotion and the skill that have gone into creating something and that's a quality I feel should be cherished.

We work with a small network of artisans. They share our values of sustainability and the need to keep their precious skills alive.

India has been such a significant and constant part of my life that it was important to me for the Bamford collection to reflect that connection in some way. And India's strong history in weaving, embroidery and printing meant that we were able to make these skills part of our story.

We work with a small network of artisans who have a distinguished heritage in textiles, in particular hand-weaving and block printing. A love and appreciation of colour permeates everything they do and gentle touches of their bright pigments infuse each of our collections. Several fabrics are woven using an ikat weave, an intricate technique native to India where the yarn is laid out in long strands, then dyed and dried to set the colour, before it is woven into a pattern by hand. The weaver must memorise the pattern and the design takes form as the yarn is woven on to the loom. From a distance the cloth might look printed but the intricacy and skill required to create the weave is astonishing; it can take months to complete a piece.

At the heart of Bamford is our relationship with nature. We strive to protect and nurture its welfare as well as considering how our own well-being is linked to the land.

THE BUTTON CUFF SWEATER

The journey and story behind this single piece sums up everything we do at Bamford. We developed the sweater with our knitwear manufacturer in the Esk Valley in Scotland. The yarn is woven from cashmere mixed with a little silk and the fabric is so fine it is like silk stockings. It is fine not simply because of how it feels on your skin but because it is precious.

Once the main panels of the sweater are knitted, the edges of the fabric start to curl inwards, so the process of stitching it together is challenging and demands great skill. The knitter must carefully thread each stitch on the seam on to the fine tooth of a large flat wheel then sew the pieces together by hand. To watch the knitters work is mesmerising: it requires enormous precision to achieve the pristine line and yet every seam on the garment is joined in this way. The buttons on the cuff are made from real akoya shell from sustainably-cultured oysters. They're sewn on upside down because I like the texture and imperfection of the rough rather than the shiny side of the shell; and in among them, you'll find a single heart-shaped button. A heart is a detail that runs right through the collection and on each piece there will be a tiny reference to it, though you may have to look hard to see it. I've always loved heart shapes – years ago I found a pebble on the beach in the shape of a heart and it's a symbol that has come to have meaning and a lot of resonance for me.

The intricacy of the knitting eventually meant that it was becoming increasingly complicated for our Scottish manufacturer to make just the small number of the sweaters we were asking for so we moved production to a small family-owned factory in Umbria. Like Scotland, the Italian textile industry is based on family-run businesses. But they too are in danger of losing this tradition due to competition from international suppliers. Simone's small factory, where we make the sweaters today, specialises in fine-gauge pieces and he still uses the machines that his father and grandfather sewed with. Working with him is a way of helping to preserve a skill and a family heritage that might otherwise be lost.

The production of conventional cotton can be harmful to workers, farmers and the environment. We source our cotton from an innovative mill that specialises in organic cotton.

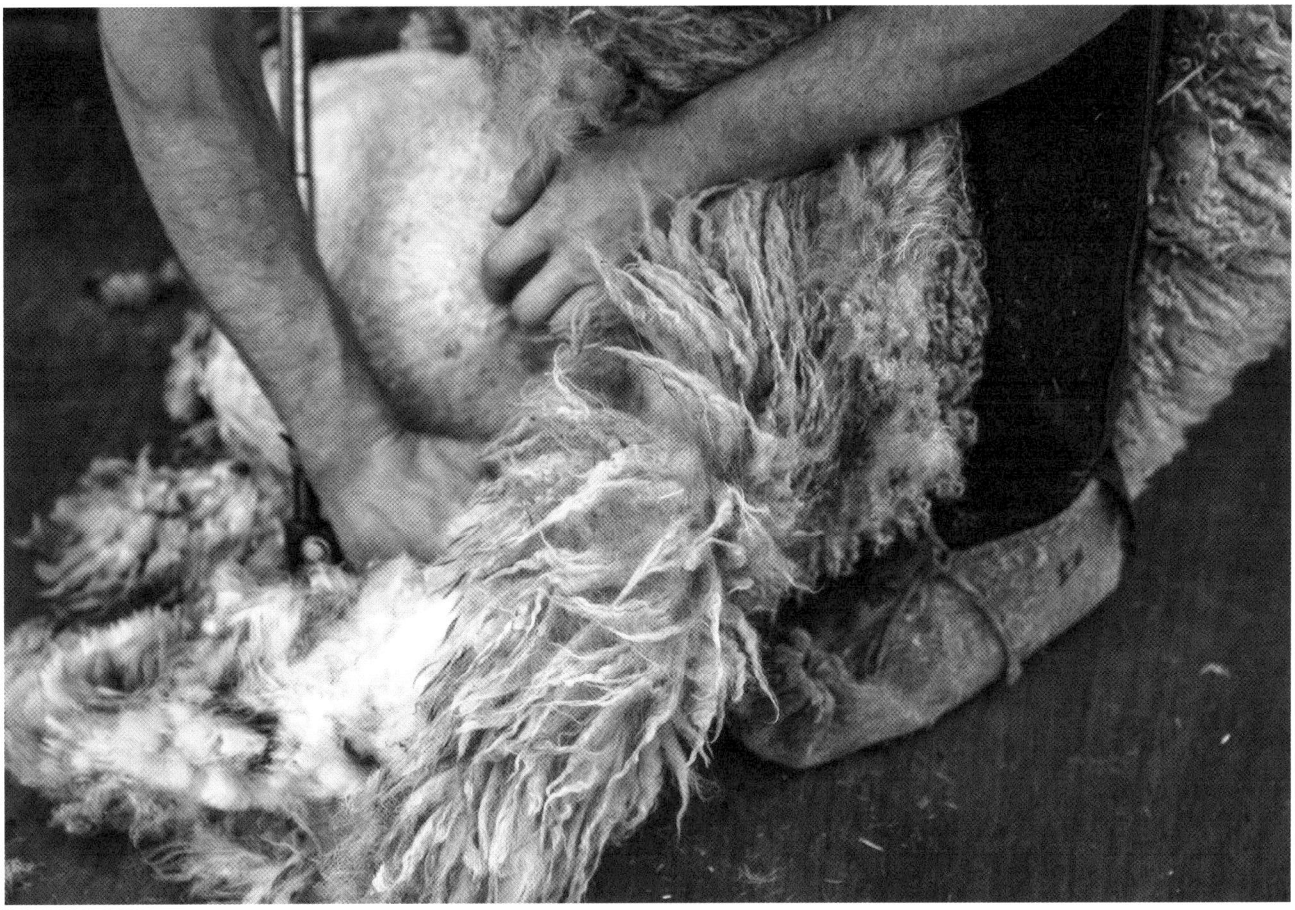

SHEEP AND WOOL

The sheep we have on the farm are all British heritage breeds. The majority of the meat we sell comes from a breed from the north of Wales called Lleyn – but some comes from our Ryelands and some from our Kerry Hills. I am particularly fond of our Ryelands. The fluffy, woolly breed is one of the oldest in England, and the sheep are known for their soft white fleeces, which produce some of Britain's finest yarns. Each year, when our sheep are shorn, their fleeces are taken to be spun locally then woven into soft throws and rugs that we sell in the shop.

And our pedigree flock of Kerry Hill sheep is very striking. Their sweet little faces with their panda eyes and black noses, ears and little black knees really are eye-catching and always get a smile from visitors to the farm.

SOURCING AND WORKING WITH ARTISANS

I value work of the hand. I get excited by craftsmanship and if somebody's gone to the trouble of making something – whether it's a scarf they've knitted or a loaf they've baked – I really appreciate the skill and the care that have gone into that craft.

Wherever I am, I'll try and seek out local artisans – here in the Cotswolds, up in Staffordshire and whenever I travel. It's partly to find things for my own home but largely to find artisans who might be able to work with us at Daylesford.

One of the most memorable, special experiences I've had was travelling to Japan to work with a master potter. We sought him out to design ceramics for a homeware and tea range we wanted to create for Bamford.

Japan fascinates me. I respect and admire its attitudes and aesthetics and they have had a huge influence on my own. There is a profound grace and a purity to the Japanese aesthetic but above all a simplicity. I spoke about their culture of wabi-sabi on page 100 and their embrace of the organic. I like faults; like the Japanese I find joy in imperfection and that's largely why I turned to Japan when we were looking to work with an artisan potter.

A master potter creates a prototype model for a ceramicist to follow and a few members of my design team and I had the privilege of spending a day with our wonderful potter at his house. We took him ideas and sketches and things that I liked; and then described how we wanted each piece to look. He sketched the piece and then we looked at his sketch and amended it together. There is a precision and focus in the process that I find mesmerising. The potter is intent upon achieving your vision for something and the result of all his work is that you have a shape that is completely unique to you.

But aside from the skills themselves, there is a wonderful sense of community and sharing that comes from artisan work. People train each other and that remains a dear yet dying quality in today's fast-paced world. Our cheesemaker, for example, will pass on his knowledge – his apprentices will become artisans themselves, ensuring that the profession lives on. Yet the renaissance of certain artisan trades and producers shows that there is a wider interest in traditional skills. We have a hedge layer come to our Summer Festival at Daylesford every year and it's exciting to see people's responses to it – there's a fascination and respect for his craft.

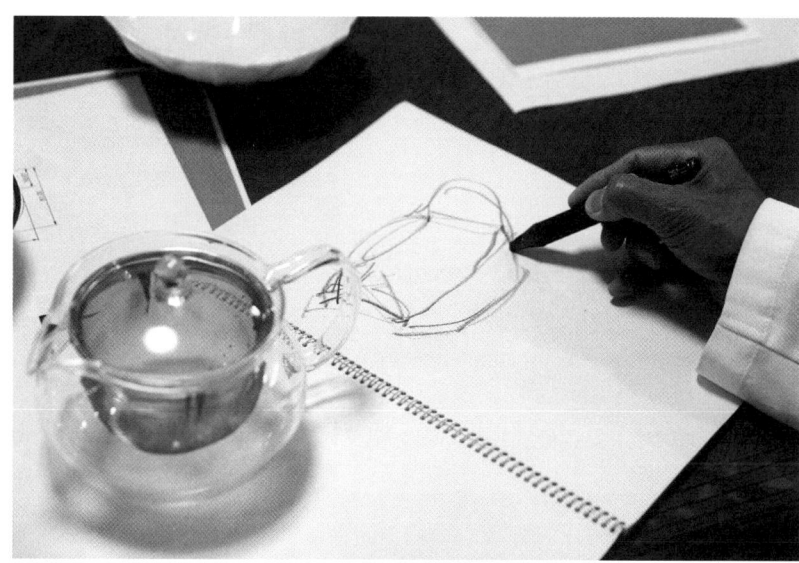

THE WILD RABBIT

I didn't mean to buy a pub. I didn't have a clue about how to run one but the owners kept calling me, insisting that it would be a wonderful idea because visitors to the farm would have somewhere to stay and be looked after in the village.

I went to see it and simply thought, 'Well, it's a beautiful building.' When I got home I told my husband I was thinking of buying it and his response was: 'What do you know about pubs – you wouldn't know what to do with it?' And that was it; the gauntlet was laid down and I decided I'd give it a go.

I think that if you analyse what everybody else does or try to mimic what's gone before you lose your innocence, your own sense of what might work and, above all, I think you lose your bravery. So I decided to stick to my instincts and try doing what I liked – to bring to my new pub what I wanted to see in a local village pub.

A modern British inn

My aim in opening The Wild Rabbit was to create a space and an atmosphere that was immediately welcoming, a convivial place to come and enjoy a drink or a meal by the fire, or the sunny pub garden in the summer. Above all I wanted to ensure that the sense of community and character that had been created by the previous owners lived on.

Constructed in local Cotswold stone, the Tollgate Inn had been a beautiful eighteenth-century building. It was important that we kept the feeling of warmth that this leant the space but also open it out a little to let in more natural light.

The original timber framework and floorboards were carefully preserved by the small team of craftsmen who carried out the work, as were the log fireplaces that have become focal points for the downstairs space. On one side of the bar is a wide raised fireplace that sits in an inviting nook, while at the opposite end the unusual double-sided fireplace allows you to see through it into the snug behind.

At the back is the more contemporary-looking dining room, a bustling, light space. In keeping with its surroundings the kitchen serves a modern British menu. There are a few nods to classic pub food, but above all the menu is inspired by the best seasonal produce from local farmers. Many of the ingredients are picked daily from our market garden.

It was important to me that the relaxed atmosphere was extended into the bedrooms so that they felt inviting and homely. I like to give rooms a sense of place or a feeling that they've been lived in. Much of this comes from recycling and reusing furniture, but also from the fabrics and textures I choose – always natural fibres such as linens, wool and leather.

We designed each bedroom at The Wild Rabbit individually, taking inspiration from the pub's history and being mindful of it, and using materials that reflected our surroundings in the Cotswolds. Antiques were sourced to fit each room's space: eighteenth-century winged shepherd's chairs are snug enough to sit in the narrow spaces and pitched ceilings

typical of tavern rooms, while much of the furniture is made from local wood. Rounds of untreated oak trunks have been turned into lamps or stools. Chestnut branches become bedposts and reclaimed apple crates have been turned into cupboards. I'm very particular about detail, so everything, right down to the lighting and rugs underfoot, has been carefully considered and sourced as locally as possible. Wool from our sheep was spun and woven into throws for the beds and vintage linens have been dyed in Gloucestershire using natural dyes then made into curtains, cushions and throws and used for upholstering antique chairs.

SEASONAL
HIGHLIGHT
CROPS FROM THE
MARKET GARDEN

MARCH
forced rhubarb
mustard greens
sea kale
spinach
sprouting broccoli

APRIL
chives
foraged wild garlic
mint
pea shoots
rhubarb
spring greens
spring onions
tarragon

MAY
lettuces
mangetout
radishes
rocket
salad leaves
sorrel
spring onions

Through the winter the beehives are quiet but as the dark days start to lengthen and there's the first glimmer of sunlight, you might start to see one or two bees popping out of their hives, and for me that's the first sign that spring is on its way. You can sense an awakening, and nature is starting to make its presence felt again.

For me, spring is all about rebirth. It means hope and new life, and as I take my early morning walk around my garden that is when I can start to see those signs. The little white snowdrops pushing their heads up towards the light is the first indication that winter really is drawing to its close. They're followed by the bright glow of the aconites which bring a welcome splash of colour to the garden after the relative barren of the winter, then comes the hardy spring cyclamen, the wild violets and the cowslips. Green shoots and fresh buds start to appear and the colour of the grass takes on a freshness and turns a beautiful bright green and you know that spring has arrived. And as we progress through the season and the days become warmer, the lambing season begins. Lambing is always a joyful time on the farm; it's something I look forward to every year and I love taking my grandchildren down to the pens in our birthing sheds to watch the lambs being born.

Spring is a time to reconnect with my senses: there's the fragrance of the garden and the spring bulbs and flowers; I particularly love the scented iris and wild violets – and it's coming up to Easter so it's also a time I think of as a period of reflection, a time to show gratitude.

The kitchen offers much to celebrate too. Brighter days bring fresher verdant flavours. The first purple sprouting broccoli is always exciting. And early on in the spring I'm looking out for Jersey Royals – there's nothing more delicious than serving them very simply with lots of fresh mint and our creamy butter. And I love the crunch and the freshness of early spring cabbage in salads.

Wild garlic can be foraged from as early as February and early March and used in so many ways – lightly sautéed on top of salmon, on pizzas, made into a pesto (turn to pages 75, 136 and 139 for our recipes); and I'll pick broad beans, peas and their pea shoots, eating them raw straight out of their pods for breakfast. And of course, there's the much anticipated arrival of the first asparagus.

SNOWDROPS
FEBRUARY

The air may still be crisp as the first snowdrop buds push their way up through the frozen soil, but the fragile white flowers are the garden's first sign that winter is behind us; there's hope around the corner and spring is on its way. In fact the colder and greyer the weather, the longer you are likely to see snowdrops; in a warm year, their appearance can be fleeting.

I collect and grow different varieties of snowdrops. There are hundreds of different kinds, some quite rare and difficult to find, but I love to hunt out the ones I haven't seen before.

Every year I like to celebrate the arrival of the first snowdrops, which are also known as the flower of hope, and signal a particularly joyful time of the year for me. A walk around the garden with my grandchildren is something we do together every year if we can: the white carpet never fails to delight them and we'll gently lift little clumps of flowers with their bulbs. And I'll always try and mark this point in the year by having friends and family round to a lunch where I'll decorate the table using the bulbs that I've lifted. I do bring snowdrops inside; some people say it's unlucky but I've never thought that and I love the purity and the freshness that the white and green bring to a table.

Snowdrops make a beautiful and simple decoration for the table and the wonderful thing about them is that you can put them back in the garden. I never pick them by cutting them — I carefully lift the plants then put them in an organic general-purpose compost in a container well lined with stones at the bottom of the pot for drainage. I like the greenery that moss adds to the pot, but it also helps prevent moisture being lost from the stems so try to add some if you have any. Snowdrops can survive for about two weeks out of the ground and then I put them back where I found them. Set on top of a crisp white linen tablecloth, with white crockery, linen napkins and perhaps a hint of green glassware, the brightness and purity of a tabletop dressed with snowdrops marks the end of winter and gives you fresh hope for the new season.

SPRING • SERVES 4

Asparagus with salsa verde

The sight of the first asparagus spears poking their heads up from the ground marks the start of a fleeting season during which I will try and enjoy those precious weeks by eating the green stems as often as I can. Asparagus is best served simply so as not to overpower its delicate flavour, which is why for me the traditional combinations remain the most successful. Served warm with the classic hollandaise overleaf is still one of my favourite ways to eat it but this light, fresh herb salsa makes for a refreshing change as the season progresses, as does the risotto on page 139. Failing that, drenching the spears in butter is never going to disappoint.

20 asparagus spears
20g parsley, roughly chopped
15g chervil, roughly chopped
10g tarragon, roughly chopped
50g capers, rinsed and chopped
1 banana shallot, roughly chopped

1 tsp Dijon mustard
60ml olive oil
4 radishes, sliced
zest of 1 lemon
salt and pepper
edible flower, to garnish (optional)

Bend the lower stems of the asparagus spears until the woody ends snap off, then use a vegetable peeler to peel the ends of the stems. Bring a wide pan of water to the boil, add the asparagus and simmer for about 5 minutes, then drain and plunge quickly into iced water and drain again well. Leave to cool.

Put the herbs, capers, shallot and mustard into a food processor and process until fairly smooth. Add the olive oil and process briefly, then check for seasoning.

To serve scatter the asparagus spears with the sliced radishes, lemon zest and edible flowers, if using. Spoon the salsa verde alongside.

SPRING • SERVES 4

Purple and white asparagus with purple sprouting broccoli and hollandaise

250g unsalted butter
4 medium egg yolks
1 tsp white wine
1 tsp white wine vinegar
8 purple asparagus spears

8 white asparagus spears
450g purple sprouting broccoli,
    ends and coarse leaves removed
salt

Melt the butter in a pan and skim any white solids from the surface. Meanwhile, whisk the egg yolks with the wine and vinegar and a little salt in a heatproof bowl. Set the bowl over a pan of simmering water and whisk until thick, about 5 minutes. Remove from the heat and slowly whisk in the melted butter until it is incorporated into the hollandaise.

Bend the lower stems of the asparagus spears until the woody ends snap off, then use a vegetable peeler to peel the end of the stems. Bring a wide pan of water to the boil, add the asparagus and simmer for about 5 minutes, then drain and plunge quickly into iced water and drain again well. Cook the sprouting broccoli in boiling water for 3–4 minutes. Drain and rinse quickly in iced water and drain again well. Arrange the warm asparagus and broccoli on a serving plate and serve with the hollandaise.

Radishes, fresh peas, butter and salt

This is a serving suggestion more than a recipe but I had to include it as it's something I have almost every day throughout the radish and pea season. Eaten straight out of the pod, fresh peas are sweet and irresistible. They're something I'll often put out alongside a starter or serve with drinks before lunch as they always look beautiful served on a board with a pile of crunchy radishes ready to be dipped in butter and salt.

20 fresh pea pods
40 radishes (use different varieties, such as long
    breakfast radishes)

125g unsalted butter, at room temperature
sea salt flakes

Split the pea pods open to reveal the peas but leave them in the pods. Wash the radishes and discard any wilted leaves. Leave the roots and leaves intact, but trimmed where necessary. On a wooden board or serving platter, arrange the prepared vegetables with any of the trimmed radish leaves. Serve with the butter to dip the vegetables in, along with sea salt flakes.

SPRING • SERVES 6–8

Spring green minestrone

A twist on the tomato-based soup, this uses the best of the season's green vegetables — beans, courgettes, peas and broad beans. Full of nutrients, the bone broth also packs it with flavour and a hit of goodness. The soup rides and falls on the flavour of the broth. I like a chicken broth as it makes use of leftover bones from a Sunday roast, but you could also use a homemade or good-quality vegetable stock. It's a versatile recipe so you can really use whatever vegetables you like — just adjust them according to what you have in your garden or what's in season at the shops.

2 tbsp olive oil
225g spinach, washed
225g rocket, washed
1 onion, diced
2 celery sticks, diced
2 courgettes, diced
2 leeks, trimmed, washed and diced
180g green beans, trimmed and diced
1.2 litres chicken bone broth or good-quality vegetable stock

bouquet garni (sprig of parsley, bay leaf and sprig of thyme tied with string)
100g peas
100g broad beans, tough skins removed
juice of ½ lemon
salt and pepper
Wild Garlic Pesto (see page 139) or regular shop-bought or homemade pesto, to serve

Heat the olive oil in a pan and wilt the spinach and rocket. Remove from the pan, cool and roughly chop. Add the onion to the same pan with the celery and cook for about 10 minutes until softened, then add the courgettes, leeks and beans and sauté for 5 minutes.

Pour in the stock and add the bouquet garni, bring to a simmer and cook for 5 minutes, then add the peas and broad beans. Add the wilted spinach and rocket with the lemon juice and check for seasoning.

Serve in warmed bowls with a spoonful of pesto on top of each.

SPRING • SERVES 4

Dressed crab with shaved asparagus

Provided we shop responsibly and find out how it's caught, British crab is one of the most sustainable forms of seafood. That's a very lucky thing for me as I love its sweet, delicate flavour. While crab is very versatile, I'm a traditionalist and I think it's hard to beat the simple flavours when it's lightly dressed with mayonnaise and plenty of lemon and black pepper. Not everyone likes the brown meat, finding its earthy flavour a little strong, so this recipe separates the two. And while something fresh and green, like this raw asparagus salad, makes a lovely accompaniment, I confess all I think the dish needs is plenty of sourdough toast, good butter, some spring sunshine and a glass of crisp white wine or rosé.

400g brown crabmeat
20g fresh white breadcrumbs
juice of 2 small lemons
2 tsp Worcestershire sauce
dash of Tabasco
1 heaped tbsp capers, rinsed and chopped
200g good-quality mayonnaise

400g white crabmeat
225g asparagus, washed and trimmed
50g baby spinach, washed
2 tbsp extra virgin olive oil
salt and pepper
sourdough bread and lemon wedges, to serve

Check carefully through the brown crabmeat, discarding any pieces of shell. Mix together with the breadcrumbs, half the lemon juice, the Worcestershire sauce, Tabasco and chopped capers. Season with salt and pepper, then place in the fridge until ready to serve. If the mixture is too thick, stir through a tablespoon of the mayonnaise.

Go through the white crabmeat in the same way, discarding any pieces of shell. Fold in the mayonnaise and remaining lemon juice. Taste and adjust the seasoning, then place in the fridge until ready to serve.

Using a mandolin or vegetable peeler, shave the raw asparagus spears into long slices. Mix with the baby spinach and drizzle with the olive oil.

Place the chilled white crabmeat in an empty crab shell or serving dish. Place the brown crabmeat mixture in a separate serving dish and serve with the asparagus salad, hunks of sourdough bread and lemon wedges for squeezing over.

SPRING • SERVES 4

Jersey Royal salad with smoked trout and tarragon mayonnaise

I'm always excited by the first sign of those fragile golden skins. While all spring new potatoes are wonderful, the delicate flavour of a real Jersey Royal cannot be beaten. They are also a regional speciality I think Britain should be very proud of. They're local (mainland Britain is the only place outside Jersey where you can buy them), and very seasonal – you can only buy them for a few weeks, so I'd encourage you to enjoy their short existence. I like mine very simply cooked with lots and lots of butter and fresh mint or a simple olive oil dressing, but they're such a special part of the spring that I've included a few recipes. Here, they give this simple salad a lovely bite.

16 Jersey Royal potatoes, halved if large
2 Little Gem lettuces, leaves torn
300g hot smoked trout, flaked
juice of 2 lemons
1 tsp tarragon, chopped
olive oil, to drizzle

FOR THE TARRAGON MAYONNAISE
2 medium egg yolks
1 tsp Dijon mustard
1 tbsp lemon juice
pinch of salt
250ml rapeseed oil
1 heaped tbsp chopped tarragon leaves
2 heaped tsp chopped mint leaves

First make the mayonnaise. Put the egg yolks into a bowl with the mustard, lemon juice and a pinch of salt. Whisk to amalgamate and then, whisking all the time, add the rapeseed oil very slowly until the mixture thickens. If it is too thick at the end, add a touch of hot water to loosen it.

Transfer 125ml of the mayonnaise to a bowl and add the chopped tarragon and mint (the rest will keep covered in the fridge for up to a week).

Bring a large pan of water to the boil and add the potatoes. Cook until tender, about 15 minutes, then drain and leave to cool.

Place the Little Gem, potatoes and flaked trout in a salad bowl. Just before serving add the lemon juice, chopped tarragon and a drizzle of olive oil; toss gently to combine. Serve with the herb mayonnaise.

SPRING • SERVES 4

Grilled sardines with tomato and caper sauce and saffron aïoli

There's a lot to recommend sardines: they're full of essential fatty acids and nutrients, sustainable, and if you're careful how you source them, they're fished in UK waters. That said, lots of people are put off buying fresh ones because of the strong smell. I think the key is to cook and eat them outdoors. Failing that, or if you're not put off by the smell, I love these simply mashed on toast with a dollop of the aïoli or tomato sauce on top.

16 new potatoes (such as Jersey Royals)
50g unsalted butter
2–3 tbsp olive oil
4 wild garlic leaves, chopped
8 sardines, deboned, tail left on (ask your fishmonger to do this for you)

FOR THE TOMATO AND CAPER SAUCE
2 tbsp olive oil
2 onions, chopped
2 garlic cloves, crushed
50g capers, rinsed
1 x 400g tin chopped tomatoes
60g butter
2 tbsp chopped parsley
salt and pepper

FOR THE SAFFRON AÏOLI
2 medium egg yolks
2 tsp Dijon mustard
1 garlic clove, crushed
200ml sunflower oil
200ml olive oil
juice of ½ lemon
small pinch of saffron threads, soaked in a teaspoon of warm water

First make the tomato sauce. Heat the olive oil in a pan over a medium heat and soften the onion and garlic for about 10 minutes. Add the capers and the tomatoes and simmer over a low heat for about 20 minutes until thickened (add a little water if it gets too thick). Stir through the butter and parsley and check for seasoning.

Next make the aïoli. Put the egg yolks, mustard and garlic in a food processor and whizz briefly just to combine. Mix the sunflower and olive oils together in a jug. With the motor running, add the oils slowly through the feeder tube until the sauce comes together and thickens. Stir in the lemon juice and the saffron mixture and check for seasoning.

Cook the potatoes in boiling water for about 15 minutes, then drain and set aside. Melt the butter in a frying pan over a medium heat. Cut the potatoes in half and, when the butter is foaming, add a splash of olive oil and sauté the potatoes until golden and crisp around the edges. Toss with the wild garlic leaves.

Meanwhile, lay the sardines on a grill rack, brush with olive oil and grill for about 5 minutes on each side.

Serve the sardines with the potatoes, tomato sauce and aïoli.

SPRING • SERVES 4

Asparagus risotto with wild garlic pesto

If you want to ring the changes with your asparagus and serve it warm, I think a risotto makes a lovely light supper, and still shows off the asparagus's delicate flavour. You could use a shop-bought pesto if you want to save on time or can't get hold of wild garlic, but if I would like a really simple meal I find the risotto is perfect just on its own.

200g asparagus spears, woody ends snapped off, cut into 3cm lengths
80g butter
1 tbsp olive oil, plus extra for drizzling
1 small onion, finely chopped
3 garlic cloves, crushed
400g risotto rice
125ml white wine
1.2 litres hot vegetable stock
60g spinach leaves, finely shredded
80g Parmesan, grated, plus shavings to garnish

salt and pepper
20g pea shoots, to garnish

FOR THE WILD GARLIC PESTO (or use 150g regular pesto, shop-bought or homemade)
130g wild garlic leaves
1 garlic clove, sliced
130ml olive oil
3 tbsp dry-roasted pumpkin seeds
25g Parmesan, grated

First make the pesto: mix half the wild garlic leaves with the garlic clove and olive oil and leave to stand for 10 minutes, then add to a food processor or blender and blitz to a smooth paste. Add the remaining leaves with the pumpkin seeds and Parmesan and pulse for a few seconds until you have a coarse pesto. Taste and season as necessary.

Bring a wide pan of water to the boil, add the asparagus and simmer for about 5 minutes, then drain and plunge quickly into iced water and drain again well. Leave to cool.

Now make the risotto. Melt half the butter and the olive oil in a wide-based pan. Add the onion and garlic and cook over a low-medium heat until softened but not coloured. Add the rice and cook slowly, stirring for 5 minutes. Pour in the white wine and reduce until the liquid has evaporated. Gradually add the hot stock, a ladleful at a time, stirring constantly. When most of the stock is absorbed, add the asparagus and spinach with the remaining butter and grated Parmesan. Stir in the wild garlic pesto and season to taste.

Serve, garnished with pea shoots, Parmesan shavings and a drizzle of olive oil.

EASTER
APRIL

Easter is a very special and significant time of year for me and I look forward to it every year. I think of it as the most important religious date in the year and wherever I am in the world I will go to church on Good Friday and Easter Sunday. As much as it is a time to celebrate new life, particularly the births that are happening on the farm, for me it is also a time for reflection and for showing gratitude for what we are blessed with in life. I'll always give up something for Lent, or take up something, as a way of acknowledging and marking that gratitude.

Tradition is important to me; I firmly believe in trying to maintain it so as a family we continue to observe some of the customs and activities that we've done since my children were very small. And it's funny how I now watch them instilling the same rituals at home with their own children and making them part of their family lives too.

When I'm at home, we will start the day early by going to church and then come home to have fresh farm eggs for breakfast. There will always be an Easter egg hunt for my grandchildren – we'll hide chocolate eggs for them in the garden and everybody dresses up with bunny ears to go and seek them out. And later we'll all sit down to a big roast lunch. It's usually lamb – not spring lamb but a leg of hogget – or sometimes we'll have chicken. And it's always served with all the best of the season's trimmings – Jersey Royals, asparagus, if it's arrived, and a rich gravy. It's a big celebration with lots of family and friends and it's really important to me that the table looks festive. Sometimes I'll have ceramic chicks and bunnies on the table, and I'll always dress it with flowers: spring bulbs; some wild daffodils; and depending on when Easter falls that year maybe lily of the valley or some wild violets. And everybody gets to take a little gift home.

Simnel cake is also an important marker for me because of its symbolism; the balls of marzipan on the top, though more of a recent addition to the traditional recipe, represent 11 of Jesus's apostles, excluding Judas. We'll always have a slice of the almondy, fruit cake with tea in the afternoon. Depending on the weather we might even make it a picnic tea.

SPRING • SERVES 6–8

Leg of hogget with parsley crust, greens and buttered potatoes

There's a tradition at Easter of eating 'spring' lamb but in reality, the lamb available is not spring lamb at all. Lambs are only just being born around Easter time so when you buy so-called spring lamb, you will be buying meat from animals that were born in the autumn; they will have had to be fattened indoors very quickly, or imported. Hogget is lamb that is a year old. It will have been born the previous spring and will have led a longer and happier life outdoors, feeding on nutritious summer pasture. The meat is darker and full of flavour. It's a stronger taste than young lamb so if my grandchildren are with me for Easter lunch, we'll usually opt for roast chicken as it's too strong for them, but hogget does make a wonderful centerpiece at a lunch for friends, perfectly matched by seasonal green vegetables and minty buttery potatoes.

2kg leg of hogget
1 tbsp olive oil
1.5kg new potatoes, washed and halved if large
sprig of mint
knob of butter
1kg purple sprouting broccoli, trimmed and washed
40 asparagus spears
salt and pepper

FOR THE PARSLEY CRUST
30g unsalted butter
200g shallots, peeled weight, finely chopped
zest and juice of 2 lemons
8 tbsp flat-leaf parsley, chopped
2 cloves of garlic crushed
2 tbsp olive oil

Preheat the oven to 220°C/gas 7. Calculate the cooking time for the hogget at 15 minutes per 450g for rare, 20 minutes for medium and 25 minutes for well done.

Put the meat into a roasting tray and rub all over with the olive oil and season with salt and pepper. Place the tray in the oven for 10 minutes then reduce the oven temperature to 180°C/gas 4 and roast for the calculated time, basting occasionally with the pan juices. When cooked to your liking remove from the oven and rest for at least 15 minutes before carving.

While the meat is cooking prepare the vegetables and parsley crust. Put the potatoes in a pan of lightly salted water, with the sprig of mint. Bring to the boil and simmer for 10–15 minutes until tender. Drain well, then tip into a serving dish, dot with butter and keep warm.

To make the parsley crust, melt the butter in a small saucepan and cook the shallots, covered, for about 15 minutes until softened. Let them cool before stirring in the lemon zest and juice, parsley, garlic and olive oil. Season to taste and spread over the rested hogget before carving.

Cook the purple sprouting broccoli in boiling water for 3–4 minutes, until just tender. (Alternatively it can be steamed.) At the same time, bend the lower stems of the asparagus spears until the woody ends snap off, then use a vegetable peeler to peel off the end of the stems. Simmer in a wide pan for about 5 minutes, before draining well.

Serve the hogget with the buttered new potatoes, broccoli and asparagus.

SPRING • SERVES 6

Panna cotta with poached rhubarb, blood orange and ginger

Panna cotta is a wonderfully light way to end a meal, but if time is short you could serve the rhubarb and oranges on their own with just some thick yoghurt or cream. I also love the rhubarb mixed with a little orange zest for breakfast.

unsalted butter, for greasing
400ml double cream
100ml full-fat milk
2 vanilla pods, split lengthways and seeds scraped out
zest of 2 oranges
100g caster sugar
3 gelatine leaves, soaked in cold water for 5 minutes

FOR THE POACHED RHUBARB
250g caster sugar
1 vanilla pod, split lengthways
6 rhubarb sticks, washed and cut into 2cm pieces

TO SERVE
3 blood oranges, peeled, pith removed and segmented
2 pieces of candied stem ginger, thinly sliced

Lightly grease six 150ml ramekins.

Put the cream into a heavy-based pan with the milk, vanilla seeds, orange zest and sugar. Slowly bring to the boil. Once boiling, remove from the heat. Squeeze any excess water out of the gelatine leaves and then add them to the pan. Stir until the gelatine dissolves, then strain the mixture into a jug. Divide the liquid between the ramekins and chill until set – this will take several hours, so it's best to do it overnight.

To poach the rhubarb, make a syrup by combining 500ml water with the sugar and vanilla pod in a large pan. Bring to the boil and stir until the sugar is dissolved. Reduce the heat and simmer for 2 minutes. Add the prepared rhubarb and simmer until tender, about 3 minutes, then remove with a slotted spoon and leave to cool.

To turn out the panna cotta, briefly dip the base of each ramekin in hot water and turn out onto serving plates. Arrange some poached rhubarb, blood oranges and the sliced stem ginger around each set cream and serve immediately.

Come April time, bluebells will start to appear across the UK's woodlands, carpeting them with an intense blue and purple, and creating one of nature's most striking spectacles. It's one of my favourite moments of the season and the perfect time to get outside for a long walk; the days feel warmer and you know that summer is just around the corner.

SUMMER

BEGINNING OF THE SEASON FROM THE MARKET GARDEN

JUNE
broad beans
cucumber
gooseberries
new potatoes
peas
radishes
salad leaves
strawberries
wet garlic

JULY
baby carrots
beetroot
blackcurrants
cherries
courgettes and flowers
cucumber
garlic
green beans
heritage tomatoes
new potatoes
salad onions
strawberries

AUGUST
aubergines
basil
broccoli
chard
dwarf French beans
green peppers
heritage tomatoes
jostaberries
morello cherries
plums
raspberries
redcurrants
runner beans

English summertime is perhaps best evoked through its food: cucumbers, peas, tomatoes and strawberries. The Jersey Royals have gone but little English new potatoes are still thriving, and I always look forward to gooseberries at this time of year. Gooseberries are so quintessentially English and I love their gentle tartness, which mellows a little when they're just very lightly poached.

Towards the end of May the countryside lanes and hedgerows around the farm are lined with lacey white cow parsley and in the garden the yellow Banksian roses are really the first sign that summer is coming. Summer gardens are also heavy with fragrance: there are the last of the daphnes, then the scented viburnum, camellias, cornflowers and sweet peas, which hang heavy in the heat. And in the early summer the elderflowers and first strawberries arrive. I love bringing summer flowers indoors – lilies can scent my whole house, and there's no need to cut them, I just bring them in in pots.

Summer is all about slowing down. It's about cherishing the warm days, getting outside to feel the sun on your face, and taking the time to enjoy the colours, sounds and smells that mark this time of the year. I try to be outside as much as possible. I'll eat in the garden three times a day if I can, practise my morning yoga and meditation on the grass, and linger outside in the evening to watch the sky as the sun sets – the colours of the sunset a different tapestry each day.

SUMMER • SERVES 4–6

Tomato consommé

This recipe is one of the dishes that best sums up the way I like to eat: it places a very seasonal ingredient centre stage and lets the flavours shine. The soup is beautifully clean-tasting and fresh – a wonderful celebration of summer's tomatoes.

2kg very ripe tomatoes, roughly chopped
2 celery sticks, roughly chopped
1 cucumber, roughly chopped
1 red onion, roughly chopped
2 tbsp olive oil
1 tsp Tabasco
2 tsp Worcestershire sauce
1 tbsp celery salt

TO GARNISH
½ cucumber, deseeded and finely diced
½ courgette, deseeded and finely diced
½ red pepper, deseeded and finely diced
½ yellow pepper, deseeded and finely diced
20 broad beans, blanched and outer skins removed
20 basil leaves, torn
olive oil, to drizzle

Put the chopped tomatoes, celery, cucumber and red onion into a food processor and pulse until you have a rough purée. Mix in the olive oil, Tabasco, Worcestershire sauce and celery salt.

Set a jelly bag or sieve lined with muslin over a bowl and pour the mixture into it, allowing it to drip overnight into the bowl. The next day, throw away the pulp and sieve the consommé once more.

Serve the soup chilled with everyone adding their own garnish and drizzling over a little olive oil.

SUMMER • SERVES 4–6

Heritage tomato salad with tapenade

I have always had huge admiration for the French attitude to food. The French take the time to sit down and enjoy their meals. Mealtimes are occasions to socialise and celebrate what you're eating with family or friends. And while there's a side to French cooking that's very elaborate and fussy, the principle at the heart of everything they do is to treat ingredients with the utmost respect; they're just as happy enjoying an elegant duck à l'orange, as they are getting stuck into a board of charcuterie served with a hunk of baguette. This simple salad is inspired by some of the salads I've eaten in Provence using their classic flavours. It's perfect on a warm summer's day with a glass of chilled rosé.

500g heritage tomatoes, at room temperature
1 tbsp olive oil
2 tsp lemon juice
½ shallot, finely diced
salt and black pepper

FOR THE TAPENADE
70g green olives, pitted (55g pitted weight)
½ tbsp capers, rinsed
2 anchovy fillets
1 garlic clove, roughly chopped
3 tbsp chopped parsley
2 sprigs of thyme, leaves picked
zest and juice of ½ lemon
4 tbsp olive oil

Put all the ingredients for the tapenade into a food processor or blender and blitz until it reaches a coarse paste. Season to taste with pepper.

Slice the tomatoes, varying the way they are cut – cut some in slices and some in wedges.

Put the tomatoes on a serving dish and drizzle with the olive oil and lemon juice, then sprinkle over the shallot, season with salt and gently fold together. Drizzle over the tapenade and serve.

SUMMER • SERVES 4

Raw artichoke with anchovy and caper dressing

The dressing for this dish is based on an Italian 'vitello tonnato', a summery dish of cold veal that's served with this sauce. I love the creamy dressing but wanted to use a vegetable instead of the meat base and artichoke seemed robust enough to stand up to the strong flavours. It's a crunchy starter for a meal outside, or could be served alongside a selection of other salads for a more substantial meal.

squeeze of lemon juice
14 violet artichokes
1 tbsp capers
rocket leaves, to garnish

FOR THE ANCHOVY AND CAPER DRESSING
2 medium eggs
1 garlic clove, crushed
200ml rapeseed oil
1 tbsp Dijon mustard
juice of 1 lemon
1 tbsp capers, rinsed
30g good-quality anchovies, drained

Remove the petals from the artichokes and set aside (you can save these and steam them later to eat with vinaigrette). Use a spoon to scoop out the fluffy choke then peel the stems with a vegetable peeler. Squeeze lemon juice over the artichoke hearts to stop them discolouring.

Bring a large pan of water to the boil and cook 12 of the artichokes for 15–20 minutes, or until tender. Once cooked, drain and allow to cool. Thinly slice both the cooked and remaining two raw artichoke hearts and spread the slices over a plate.

Put all the dressing ingredients into a food processor or blender and blitz until combined. Drizzle the dressing over the artichokes and scatter with the capers. Garnish with the rocket leaves and serve.

SUMMER • SERVES 4

Cucumber salad

A glut of cucumbers is a common occurrence at the farm so we are endlessly trying to come up with new ways to serve them. This Asian-inspired salad contrasts cooling green chunks of the vegetable with a spicy sesame dressing.

1½ cucumbers
25g caster sugar
pinch of salt
40g baby leaf spinach, torn
2 heaped tbsp chopped mint leaves
2 heaped tbsp chopped coriander leaves
2 spring onions, sliced diagonally into 4cm lengths
25ml rice wine vinegar

2 tbsp sesame oil
2 tsp tamari or soy sauce
1 large garlic clove, crushed
½ red chilli, deseeded and finely chopped
small knob of fresh ginger, peeled and grated
½ tsp clear honey
1 tbsp toasted sesame seeds

Wash the cucumbers and pat dry. Trim the ends and cut in half lengthways. Lay the cucumbers on a chopping board, cut side down, and smash with a meat tenderiser or rolling pin. The cucumber will split and the seeds will come out. Discard the seeds and then cut the split cucumbers into bite-sized pieces and place in a large sieve over a bowl. Sprinkle over the sugar and salt and toss together, then weight down with something (a bag of ice cubes works well) and place in the fridge for about 4 hours.

Discard the liquid in the bowl and place the cucumbers in a serving dish. Add the spinach, mint, coriander and spring onions. Put the rice vinegar, sesame oil, tamari, garlic, chilli, ginger, honey and toasted sesame seeds into a lidded jam jar and shake well. Pour the dressing over the salad and gently stir through before serving.

SUMMER • SERVES 4–6

Summer tabbouleh

Although this salad will be familiar to many, I wanted to include a recipe because it champions humble garden herbs – parsley and mint – which are things that we can all grow at home, even on a windowsill. It's also a salad that sits very happily alongside a selection of others and works well with cold meats, fish or at a barbecue. This recipe includes quinoa as well as the traditional bulgur wheat, which gives added nutrition as well as a lovely textural contrast to the crunchier grain.

150g bulgur wheat
150g tricolour quinoa
2 tomatoes, deseeded and chopped
25g kale, tough stems removed and leaves chopped
5 tbsp chopped parsley
3 tbsp chopped mint
40ml garlic oil (see below)
juice of 1 lemon
salt and pepper

FOR THE GARLIC OIL
4 garlic cloves, halved lengthways
60ml sunflower oil
1 tsp wholegrain mustard
1 tsp lemon juice

First make the garlic oil. Preheat the oven to 160°C/gas 3. Place the halved garlic cloves in a small ovenproof dish, pour over the sunflower oil and cover the dish with foil. Cook in the oven for 25–30 minutes until the garlic is soft. Sieve the garlic and the oil into a bowl, gently pushing the cooked garlic through with a wooden spoon. Whisk the oil vigorously, gradually adding the mustard and lemon juice.

Put the bulgur wheat and quinoa into a pan, cover with water and bring to the boil. Simmer for about 10 minutes, or until tender. Drain the grains and leave to cool before putting in a serving bowl. Add the tomatoes, raw kale and herbs and fold through the garlic oil and lemon juice. Season to taste before serving.

SUMMER • SERVES 4

Roast salmon, peas, bacon and braised Little Gem

Wild salmon comes into season at the start of the summer, so this dish is based around pairing it with other seasonal ingredients. As with all seafood, do check what you're buying by consulting the Marine Stewardship Council website or talking to your fishmonger to be sure of its provenance. The accompaniment is a twist on the classic French dish, 'petit pois à la française', something I'm quite partial to, in which peas and lettuce are braised in stock and butter. My husband likes the addition of the bacon, but you could happily leave it out to make it a meat-free dish.

320g fresh peas (or use frozen)
250g new potatoes (such as Jersey Royals), halved if large
2 carrots, cut into strips
4 skin-on salmon fillets, about 160g each
60g butter
3 tbsp olive oil
80g back bacon, cut into strips
1 banana shallot, finely diced

120ml vegetable stock
240ml double cream
4 tbsp chopped parsley
4 tbsp chopped mint
2 Little Gem lettuces, outer leaves removed, quartered
salt and pepper

Blanch the peas in boiling water for 1 minute and then refresh in iced water. Drain and leave to one side.

Bring a large pan of water to the boil, add the potatoes and cook until tender, about 15 minutes, adding the carrots for the last 5 minutes. Drain and set aside. Once the potatoes are cool enough to handle, peel off the skins.

Season the salmon with salt and pepper. In a frying pan over a medium heat, melt the butter and olive oil together and pan-fry the fish skin-side down for 8–10 minutes until golden brown, then turn over and cook for a further minute. Remove to a plate and cover with foil.

Fry the bacon and diced shallot in the same pan for 2 minutes, before adding the vegetable stock, double cream, potatoes, carrots and peas; bring to the boil. Add the parsley and mint and season to taste. Add the Little Gem wedges and simmer for a further 3 minutes.

To serve place two Little Gem wedges in each bowl or plate, spoon over some creamy vegetables and bacon and then place a salmon fillet on top.

SUMMER • SERVES 6

Summer cup

It really is worth taking the time to leave this to steep for the full two days. I know it might sound like a long time, but it really does make a difference to the finished flavour. When you sip the drink, it feels like you've bottled the taste of summer and the wait will have been worth it. At home this is something we'll have for an occasion — often when we have friends for a picnic or barbecue — so I can factor in the steeping time.

1 bottle of dry white wine
30ml Maraschino liqueur
30ml Grand Marnier
70ml sugar syrup
200g fresh fruit of your choice, prepared as necessary (we like pineapple, peaches, apple, mango and strawberry)

TO DECORATE
sliced strawberries
lemon and orange peel
sprigs of mint

Combine all the ingredients in a large jug and leave to marinate in the fridge for at least 2 days.

To serve, strain into ice-filled highball glasses and decorate with the sliced strawberries, lemon and orange peel and mint sprigs.

EATING OUTDOORS
JULY

Why is it that everything tastes better outside? I can't think of a better way to spend a summer's day than enjoying a picnic on the lawn with my family and friends, surrounded by summer blossoms, the sound of the bees buzzing and the scent of herbs warmed by the sun.

I adore everything about picnics. I love the simplicity of the food: piles of crunchy raw vegetables with dips, some crusty bread and cheese, quiches, boiled eggs, little cucumber sandwiches and tomatoes that you bite into like apples. And there's nothing better than a fresh summer radish.

When friends and family are round I'll often set up long tables in the garden. We'll have big bowls of salad, dips on boards and simple pâtés or pickled vegetables in jars. I love the sharing and interaction that comes with all the passing of food and the topping up of drinks. My grandchildren love picnics so when I'm with them we'll just find the sunniest spot and lay out picnic blankets on the lawn – cocktail sausages and their favourite sandwiches will emerge from the baskets before the rugs have barely touched the ground.

Baskets or bowls of strawberries or other summer fruits – juicy ripe peaches, raspberries and cherries – are always irresistible at a summer picnic. And then there is jelly. Perhaps there's simply a bit of nostalgia that comes with eating jelly and ice cream, but I absolutely adore jellies and I think they are particularly wonderful in the summer. They really celebrate the best of the season's ingredients and allow the purity and intensity of a flavour to shine. If I've got guests coming over I'll often use it as an excuse to make a jelly.

Eating outdoors isn't confined to summer for me; I eat outside whenever I can – in a jumper or a coat. And while I'll always choose a picnic over a barbecue, there is something so wonderfully English about that first barbecue of the year, when the first rays come out from behind the clouds and the opportunity to light the coals gets seized upon. For most it's probably still a bit too cold to be eating outside – coats will come out and the drizzle inevitably starts just as you're about to cook the sausages – but I love how the British, myself included, will all stubbornly sit outside and relish in that moment all the same.

Entertaining outside can be much easier in summer than in other months; you can bring people together in a really informal way and the table can reflect that. At the farm, we've had a few supper clubs over the summer in our market garden and it's allowed us to be more creative with the table setting. Here I've drawn inspiration from our surroundings and used hay bales as chairs. For crowds that stay past sunset putting hurricane lamps on the tables to be able to light candles is always a good idea.

CHÂTEAU LÉOUBE

Provence has always held a special allure for me – I think it's because the lavender is just breathtaking. My husband and I had been looking for a house in Provence for a while when we eventually found Léoube, our sleeping beauty.

Set back from a quiet coastal bay on the coastline, the house had been owned by the same family for years but hadn't been touched; we fell in love with it. The lady owner was very elderly and she wanted it looking after; so in a way she chose us, rather than us choosing it. Léoube was a big project. The house, gardens and a vineyard were all there but they needed somebody to love them; we had to bring them back to life.

Today the Léoube estate is where we produce our organic Provençal wines and olive oils. The vineyard had been run by our next-door neighbours, the Ott family, and when we bought the estate we asked Monsieur Ott's son to come and work for us; we call him Little Ott. Provence's mild Mediterranean climate means that it has one of the most perfect settings for winemaking. The winters are mild and the summer's dry daytime heat is tempered by the gentle but cooling night-time breezes. The occasional gust of the region's mistral wind keeps the vines aerated and dry and prevents them attracting mildew or disease.

But what I find most fascinating about Léoube is its soil. Provence is home to some of the oldest vineyards in France and the soil there dates back over 800 million years. The seabeds once sat on the estate's land, which saturated the soil with an array of minerals and means that you still get a lightly salty and refreshing finish in the wine.

To honour the history and tradition of winemaking in the area, the wine at Léoube is produced following artisan principles. The trimming of the vines, as well as the harvesting and sorting of the grapes is all carried out by hand, and their timings are guided by the solar and lunar cycles in accordance with the biodynamic calendar. The grapes are pressed immediately after harvesting to extract the juice at its freshest and it's left to ferment slowly. Nothing is added or taken away during the process and nothing is rushed.

Artisan wine changes with the season – like cheese, it tastes different every year but we're very proud of the fact that all our wines, particularly the three rosés, are consistently recognised as striking and excellent examples of their terroir. For me, the rosé is summer in a bottle.

A few years after arriving at Léoube, we decided to start producing olive oil too. We laid down 5,000 olive trees, a blend of Provençal and Italian varieties. Like the grapes, the olives are handled very delicately and carefully to harness their flavours.

We harvest using nets and gently vibrating tongs before washing them in natural spring water. The production is quite small as we only press oil from what we grow and one year we didn't have any oil at all. Because we don't use pesticides or antibiotics, one year the trees caught a bug. There was nothing we could do and we had to explain to our suppliers what had happened; that's just part of being artisan – you're dependent on nature and at the mercy of what it chooses to throw at you.

When we do have it though, the oil is a beautiful fragrant pale liquid; it smells like green bananas and it's absolutely wonderful. And when it's all sold, it's gone and we have to wait and see what the next year will bring.

SUMMER • SERVES 8

Léoube rosé jelly with summer berries

I am extremely fond of jellies. I love their shapes, which make me feel like a child again, but jellies are also full of flavour and should definitely not be confined to children's birthday parties. I serve jelly with a few options; something that pleases everyone, such as cream or ice cream, but I also like to serve it with something that enhances the main flavour — a mango sorbet or granita with a mango jelly, or a berry ice cream with a berry jelly.

1 litre Rosé de Léoube, or other dry rosé wine
275g caster sugar
3 sprigs of mint, plus extra to decorate
2 star anise
4 slices of lemon

10 gelatine leaves
200g raspberries
200g loganberries
200g tayberries

Line a 1 litre loaf tin, or similar size mould, with cling film with some overlapping the sides – this will help when turning the set jelly out.

In a small pan, gently heat the wine with the sugar, mint sprigs, star anise and lemon slices. Stir to dissolve the sugar and allow to infuse for a couple of minutes. Meanwhile soak the gelatine leaves in a small bowl of cold water. Strain the wine through a sieve and add the softened gelatine leaves to the wine, squeezing out any excess water first. Stir to dissolve.

Pour a centimetre of jelly into the lined mould and place in the fridge to set. Once set, add the berries in layers and then pour over the remaining wine mixture. Carefully return to the fridge and leave to set for at least 4–6 hours.

To serve, unmould the jelly onto a serving dish and decorate with mint sprigs.

Friends of mine often comment on how I lay my table for a dinner party. I'm not artistic but dressing a table is my way of expressing a little creativity. It's a joy for me and in turn I love seeing others enjoy it. A beautiful table makes a meal memorable. The ideas for what I'm going to use for the table always start in the garden. I come across flowers or stems on my morning walk with the dogs and I'll think about the pots or vases I want to use for them on the table. Then the linens will follow. They'll usually be white as it doesn't fight with the foliage, but sometimes there will be a hint of green or, as here, a darker colour — a blue from the embroidery just to bring in a subtle hint of colour.

BEEKEEPING AND HARVESTING HONEY

AUGUST

For as long as I can remember I have been fascinated by bees. Bees are vital for our survival. They are nature's essential pollinators and without them there would be no flowering plants or much of the food we produce.

I get very frightened by the silence of the bees and in February I watch closely for signs of activity from our hives. British bee populations have been in decline since the 1970s and there are many threats to their survival. When industrial farming began in Britain, we began to pull out most of our hedgerows and flood the fields and countryside with polluting chemicals and insecticides, which not only wiped out much of the bee population but destroyed their natural habitats too.

I have become passionate about doing everything I can to help protect and support the survival of our bees, both within the farm and by trying to spread the message beyond it. When we first turned Daylesford over to organic farming, one of the most striking changes we noticed was the return of the bees – suddenly we could hear and see them hovering over the fields again. By farming organically we are taking a first step towards supporting the bees, providing them with a healthy, hospitable habitat to go about their work. Just as we require a balanced and varied diet for our own health, bees need access to a range of nutrients so the diversity of the wild spaces around Daylesford helps us to ensure we provide a constant but changing supply of flora from which the bees can source their nectar and pollen throughout the year.

We have 40 beehives across the farm and today they are tended by a team of Daylesford staff who volunteered to look after them simply because they took an interest in their welfare. Honeybees are particularly important and efficient pollinators, partly due to the large number of forager bees in each colony, but also due to their physique and because they only forage one plant species at one time. They are also an endless source of fascination and the hives draw many curious onlookers. I take my grandchildren to the hives and they adore them. They're not frightened by them at all and love getting dressed up in the protective suits. They're also extremely quick to spot the queen bee, which is actually very difficult to do. Watching bees work is something I find captivating and it's been wonderful to watch the interest there has been in our hives both among staff and visitors.

Our honeybees are at their most active over the summer – they love the heat of the sun – so in September or early October, once the hives have an ample store of honey to share, our team goes into the hives to harvest some of it, always leaving enough so that the bees have a plentiful source of energy to see them through the winter. Our farm honey is as pure and natural as it can be, cut from the frame and immediately transferred to jars. And as soon as we put the jars on the shelves, it's gone within a week. For me the flavour of our honey is absolutely delicious, but above all the little pots on my breakfast table are the proof of our bees' hard work, a reminder of just who is responsible for ensuring our crops can grow and that we are able to enjoy nutritious food throughout the year.

When we first turned Daylesford over to organic farming, one of the most striking changes we noticed was the return of the bees – suddenly we could hear and see them hovering over the fields again.

AUTUMN

HIGHLIGHTS FROM THE MARKET GARDEN

SEPTEMBER
apples
blackberries
broccoli
celery
green cobnuts
Florence fennel
leeks
onions
plums
raspberries
red peppers
shallots
sweetcorn

OCTOBER
apples
beetroot
blackberries
broccoli
carrots
celeriac
damsons
kale
leeks
pears
potatoes
radicchio
squash
wet walnuts

NOVEMBER
apples
beetroot
celeriac
chard
jerusalem artichokes
kale
land cress
leeks
red cabbage
squash
winter black radish
winter salad leaves

I know it's autumn when the wet walnuts emerge in the woodlands. Creamy and sweet, the wet nuts are very different to the crunchy kernels that dry out over October and November and start to sit on our tables come Christmastime. Available for a fleeting few weeks, they are a truly seasonal treat and just so wonderfully, uniquely English.

Each season brings new excitements, but autumn is one of my favourite times on the farm; there's an abundance of riches from the garden. The root vegetables are being dug up from the ground: turnips, parsnips, all the different varieties of pumpkins and squashes, and the swede. The pear, plum and damson trees are heavy with fruit and all our heritage varieties of apple arrive, providing us with so many different flavours and textures. I love going into the store to see the apples all laid out on trays, labeled with their names and ready to be carefully preserved throughout the winter so that we have them for the months to come. We'll always have a glut of apples on the farm and Jez, our head gardener, turns them into a delicious tangy cider.

Autumn is a cosy season. Hats, scarves and gloves get pulled on for walks in the colder air and it's time to light the fire for the first time. But, above all, for me it's the flavours that are so comforting this season: gentle and warming yet bolstering. I love long, slow cooking – all the soups and stews and casseroles – and it's in autumn that this really comes into its own. I love stockpots. I love the simplicity of preparing a stock and all the different flavours – game, chicken, beef or vegetable – bubbling away on the stove. When I was a child, Sunday mornings after church were the time for cooking and my mother would get several pots of stock on the go. She'd put *The Archers* on in the background and we'd sit together chopping and chatting. There was something so constant about that Sunday ritual and the soothing smells drifting around the house that I still find there's something very comforting and reassuring about a simmering pot of stock.

While I mostly try to lift bulbs or plants when I bring them into my house, there are certain occasions and times of the year when I will take cuttings to make up arrangements of flowers or to use them as table decorations. I love mixing herbs, such as flowering mint, rosemary and borage, with wild flowers to give vases a wonderful aroma as well as extra greenery. And in the autumn and winter, the shapes and textures of the season's vegetables are perfect for dressing a table. I'll nestle baby cabbages in earthenware pots, place knobbly gourds on mantelpieces and wind blackberries, spruce, ivy, artichoke thistles, holly berries and elderberries around willow to make wreaths.

AUTUMN • SERVES 4

Pickled blackberries and red cabbage with chicken liver pâté

Perhaps I'm biased – since childhood my favourite pudding has been a blackberry and apple crumble – but I feel blackberries are a very underused fruit and I'd love to encourage you to make more of them. Blackberries can be used in both a sweet and a savoury context, but above all they are free and readily available to us all. As a wild fruit that grows in British hedgerows we can all go and seek them out (for information about blackberrying, see page 215). This simple means of pickling them is a nice way of preserving them without resorting to jam. The sweet–sharp pickle cuts through the richness of the pâté, and if you have any leftover pickle or want to use up more of your hedgerow forage, it pairs well with a charcuterie board or goat's cheese on toast.

1 beetroot
250ml red wine vinegar
75g caster sugar
2 sprigs of thyme
¼ red cabbage, thinly sliced
150g blackberries

4 slices of sourdough bread
160g good-quality smooth chicken liver pâté
1 green apple, cored and cut into batons
Beetroot, Apple and Ginger Chutney, to serve (see page 201)

First cook the beetroot. Remove the leaves and gently wash the beetroot – do not peel at this stage. Put into a pan, add just enough boiling water to cover and simmer for 30–40 minutes, or until tender. Drain and allow to cool a little before peeling and dicing.

Put the vinegar, sugar and thyme sprigs into a pan with 50ml water. Place over a medium heat and bring to the boil. As soon as the liquid has come to the boil, take it off the heat.

Place the sliced cabbage and blackberries in a non-metallic bowl and pour over the hot pickling liquid. Leave to cool.

Toast the slices of bread and top each with a spoonful of pâté. Garnish with the diced beetroot, apple batons, pickled blackberries and cabbage and serve with the chutney.

AUTUMN • SERVES 4

Raw cauliflower and black quinoa with spiced pumpkin seed dressing

Salads aren't generally associated with the colder weather but I eat them all year round and the crunch of a raw vegetable and bite of a grain can make a welcome change from soups and stews, particularly at lunchtime. The spices in this dressing bring a natural warmth and add punch to this light yet sustaining salad.

200g black quinoa
1 cauliflower, leaves removed, shaved on a mandolin
1 carrot, finely grated
3 tbsp chopped coriander
85g sultanas, finely chopped
1½ tbsp cider vinegar
salt and pepper

FOR THE SPICED PUMPKIN SEED DRESSING
120ml olive oil
125g onions, chopped
2 garlic cloves, chopped
1 tbsp curry powder
zest and juice of ½ lemon
½ tbsp black onion (nigella) seeds
25ml pumpkin seed oil

Rinse the quinoa well in cold water. Put in a pan with roughly double the amount of water and bring to the boil. Reduce the heat and simmer for 15–20 minutes, or until tender. Drain and cool.

To make the dressing, heat half the olive oil in a frying pan over a medium heat and sweat the chopped onion and garlic until soft and almost translucent. Add the curry powder, lemon zest and onion seeds and cook for a few more minutes, then remove from the heat. Add salt to taste then transfer to a blender and whizz until smooth. Add the remaining olive oil, the pumpkin seed oil and lemon juice, stirring well.

To serve, place the quinoa, shaved cauliflower, grated carrot, coriander and sultanas into a serving dish. Drizzle over the cider vinegar and stir through the dressing. Season to taste before serving.

AUTUMN • SERVES 4–6

Beluga lentils, squash and wild rice

Like the salad on the previous page, this is one I enjoy a lot in the colder months. It makes use of the season's winter root veg, which become wonderfully soft and sweet when roasted – a pleasing contrast to the nutty, chewy wild rice and firm lentils.

250g dried beluga lentils, soaked in cold water for 30 minutes
200g wild rice, soaked in cold water for 30 minutes
600ml boiling water
100g butternut squash, deseeded and diced
110ml olive oil, plus extra for drizzling
2½ tbsp coconut flakes
100ml balsamic vinegar

1½ tbsp clear honey
100g carrots, finely diced
1 small red pepper, deseeded and finely diced
1 red onion, finely diced
3 tbsp roughly chopped parsley
1½ tbsp roughly chopped coriander
salt and pepper

Preheat the oven to 180°C/gas 4.

Drain and rinse the lentils and rice and put into two separate pans. Cover the lentils with 500ml cold water, bring to the boil, then cover, reduce the heat and simmer for 25 minutes. Drain and set aside.

Cover the rice with the boiling water, add a pinch of salt and cook over a medium heat for 50–55 minutes, or until the grains have popped (top up with more boiling water if necessary). Remove from the heat, keeping the pan covered for a further 5 minutes, then fluff up the grains with a fork.

While the lentils and rice are cooking, put the squash into a small baking tray, drizzle with olive oil and cook in the oven for 25 minutes until crisped at the edges. Set aside to cool.

Once the squash, rice and lentils have cooled, put a frying pan over a medium heat and gently toast the coconut flakes until golden brown, being careful not to let them catch.

In a small bowl, whisk together the olive oil, vinegar and honey. Combine the rice, lentils, squash, carrots, coconut, red pepper, red onion and herbs in a large bowl and toss with the dressing. Taste and season with salt and pepper before transferring to a serving dish.

THE HERITAGE ORCHARD
SEPTEMBER

England has a long and rich heritage in growing fruit. We are the only country that has traditionally made a distinction between cooking, eating and cider apples, and traditional farm orchards often contained a mix of all three. Planting trees that produced fruit at different times and for different purposes used to provide a valuable food source for growers, and the knowledge of how to cultivate, use and store the fruit was passed down through generations. Yet with the growth of supermarket fruit, today many people's experience of apples is confined to the shiny fruit you find on shelves all year round and this precious knowledge risks being lost along with so many of our heritage apple varieties.

I didn't want to see this happen, so in 2010 I asked our garden team to cultivate a traditional orchard at the farm. Forty-eight trees were planted and it is an orchard that has been created in the most traditional sense of the word, containing a mix of old English varieties – ours are all local or regional; both eating and cooking apples. Aside from ensuring that future generations will be able to taste and enjoy these varieties of fruit, traditional orchards have been recognised as being beneficial for biodiversity and the fruit grown in well-established orchards often suffers few disease problems, both of which are central tenets of organic farming and principles that are so important to us at Daylesford.

The orchard is something I am incredibly proud of. Harvesting apples is one of the joys of the autumn and we celebrate the orchard and the apples it produces every year at our Harvest Festival. I'm also delighted to be able to share the orchard with others and provide an educational resource. The fruit we harvest is gifted to school children and farm visitors for juicing and tasting, or offered to local village fêtes and food festivals for demonstrations and sampling. Rarer specimens will provide the stock for future planting projects and orchard restoration; and happily there are still plenty left over for us to make cider.

PRESERVING • MAKES 4 x 340G JARS

Beetroot, apple and ginger chutney

Autumn is a time for harvesting but also for making sure we store and preserve that harvest so that nothing perishes and goes to waste. It's the perfect time to turn fruit and vegetables into jams and chutneys. With a large orchard at the farm, apples are something we regularly have a glut of so our chefs are often playing around with them, using different partners to create different styles. Here, the earthy yet sweet beetroot is a good match, while the ginger gives the chutney a lovely warming kick. Overleaf is my husband's favourite condiment – our table is never without a jar – and one of my favourite jams, again based around the wealth of plums I am blessed with every year.

900g raw beetroot, peeled and half diced and half coarsely grated
450g onions, chopped
450g cooking apples, peeled, cored and diced
25g fresh ginger, peeled and grated
600ml cider vinegar
350g caster sugar
salt and pepper (optional)

First, sterilise your jars. Preheat the oven to 120°C/gas ½. Wash the jars in soapy water and rinse well, then put on a baking tray in the oven for 10 minutes. Switch the oven off and leave the jars inside while you get on with the chutney.

Place everything except the sugar into a heavy-based pan. Bring to the boil then reduce the heat and simmer for 1½ hours.

Add the sugar and cook for a further 20 minutes until thickened, stirring occasionally to prevent the mixture sticking to the pan. Taste, and add seasoning if required.

Pour the chutney into the warm sterilised jars (it is important that the jars are warm, as cold ones may crack when the hot mixture is added). Seal with the lids and store in a cool, dark place, where the chutney will keep unopened for up to 12 months (once opened store in the fridge and eat within 2–3 weeks).

Piccalilli

MAKES 2 x 450G JARS

2 cauliflowers, broken into small florets
4 shallots, finely chopped
200g baby onions, peeled
600ml white wine vinegar
300ml malt vinegar
pinch of chilli flakes
1 garlic clove, halved
5 sprigs of thyme

2 tbsp coriander seeds
2 cucumbers, peeled, deseeded and diced
3 tbsp English mustard powder
2 tbsp ground turmeric
2 heaped tbsp salt, plus extra for sprinkling
125g caster sugar
2 tbsp cornflour

The day before you make the piccalilli, place the prepared cauliflower, shallots and baby onions into a large bowl and sprinkle with salt. Leave overnight. The next day, in a large pan, bring the vinegars to the boil with the chilli flakes, garlic, thyme sprigs and coriander seeds and simmer for 5 minutes. Strain and discard the chilli, garlic, thyme sprigs and coriander seeds and allow to stand for 20 minutes. Sterilise your jars (see page 201).

Lightly sprinkle the prepared cucumber with the salt and leave for 15 minutes. Rinse all the vegetables and mix together well. In a bowl mix the mustard powder, turmeric, salt, sugar and cornflour, and add a little of the cooled vinegar to make a paste. Bring the vinegar back to the boil and gradually stir in the spice paste. Simmer for 3 minutes, cool a little and then pour over the vegetables. Stir gently, until they are covered in the sauce. Pour into the warm sterilised jars and store in a cool dark place for a couple of months before eating. Once opened, keep in the fridge and eat within 2 weeks.

Plum and bitter almond jam

MAKES 4 x 350G JARS

900g (stoned weight) stoned plums
juice of ½ lemon
700g granulated sugar
1 tsp almond extract
5g flaked almonds

Sterilise your jars (see page 201). Put a saucer in the freezer, ready to test for setting point.

Place the prepared plums in a large pan with the lemon juice and 200ml cold water. Bring to the boil, then reduce the heat and cook over a low–medium heat until the plums have collapsed, about 20 minutes.

Add the sugar and stir until it has dissolved, then bring to the boil, removing any scum that rises to the top with a slotted spoon. Boil rapidly for about 10 minutes, or until setting point is reached. To test for a set remove the chilled saucer from the freezer and spoon a little jam onto it. Leave to cool a little and then push the jam with your finger; if a skin has formed (or the jam 'wrinkles') the jam has set. If not, return the saucer to the freezer and boil the jam a little longer and test again. Once setting point is reached, remove the pan from the heat and stir through the almond extract and flaked almonds. Fill your warm sterilised jars and then seal. Store in a cool, dry place for up to 12 months; once opened, keep in the fridge and eat within 3 months.

AUTUMN • SERVES 3–4

Baywell tartiflette

Daylesford has grown up around our dairy and creamery and I continue to be extremely proud of the work our team does in making and creating our artisan cheeses by hand. Named after the pastures around the farm, Baywell is our soft, rind-washed cheese, which is inspired by the irresistible Reblochon from the Alps. Baywell has a slightly more pungent, herby flavour but it makes a wonderful substitute for the traditional cheese in one of the Alps' most famous dishes. Hearty and warming, a tartiflette is my idea of heaven on a cold wintry evening, best served with a robust glass of red wine.

550g peeled potatoes (about 620g unpeeled weight), halved
knob of butter (about 15g)
1 tbsp olive oil
130g streaky bacon, finely chopped
2 small onions, thinly sliced
2 tsp thyme leaves, plus a little extra to garnish

80ml white wine
70ml chicken bone broth
70ml double cream
120g Baywell cheese, sliced
handful of rocket, to garnish
1 tbsp French dressing
salt and pepper

Preheat the oven to 180°C/gas 4.

Put the potatoes into a pan, cover with cold water and a little salt and place over a high heat. Bring to the boil and then reduce the heat and simmer until just beginning to soften, about 5 minutes. Drain well and leave to steam-dry. As soon as they are cool enough to handle, slice thinly.

Melt the butter with the olive oil in a 25cm heavy-based ovenproof frying pan. Add half the bacon and cook until golden. Add the onion slices and thyme leaves and cook for about 10 minutes until soft. Add the white wine and reduce a little, then add the chicken broth and reduce again. Finally add the double cream and simmer until you have a coating consistency. Season to taste. Fold through the potatoes, spreading them out evenly.

Fry the remaining bacon in another frying pan until golden. Sprinkle the fried bacon over the potato mix. Top with the sliced cheese and sprinkle over a few thyme leaves. Bake in the oven for about 10 minutes until it is starting to bubble around the edges.

Carefully remove the pan from the oven. Toss the rocket leaves in the dressing and use to garnish the tartiflette.

Roast cod and Jerusalem artichokes in smoked bacon broth

Fish is of course something we don't produce at the farm, so it's something I generally reserve for special occasions or dinner parties. Cod is quite a meaty, robust fish so it stands up well to this smokey broth. While there is nothing fancy about this dish's humble bacon and vegetable base, it looks quite refined and elegant with the cod loin perched on top of the veg.

3 tbsp olive oil, plus extra for frying
½ carrot, finely diced
1 small onion, finely diced
1 celery stick, finely diced
½ fennel bulb, finely diced
1 garlic clove, crushed
60g smoked bacon lardons
100ml white wine
2 sprigs of thyme

300ml chicken bone broth
700g Jerusalem artichokes, peeled and quartered
500g floury potatoes, peeled and halved
4 thick-cut cod loins (about 200g each)
60ml double cream
75g unsalted butter, softened
1 tbsp finely chopped chives
2 tbsp chopped parsley
salt and pepper

Heat a tablespoon of olive oil in a deep frying pan over a medium heat and cook the carrot, onion, celery and fennel until softened but not coloured, about 15 minutes. Add the garlic, bacon lardons, wine, thyme sprigs and chicken broth and cook until reduced by half. Season with salt and pepper, set aside and keep warm.

Preheat the oven to 180°C/gas 4.

Bring a large pan of water to the boil and cook the Jerusalem artichokes until al dente, about 10 minutes, then drain well and refresh under cold water. Transfer the artichokes to a roasting tray, toss with the remaining olive oil and roast for 35–40 minutes, or until golden.

Meanwhile, cook the potatoes in boiling salted water until soft, about 15–20 minutes.

Heat a splash of olive oil in a frying pan and fry the cod loins until lightly coloured, about 2 minutes on each side, then place in the oven with the artichokes for the last 8–10 minutes of cooking time.

Drain the potatoes and then mash until smooth, then beat in the cream and butter. Garnish with the chives. Stir the chopped parsley into the bacon broth.

Serve the cod steaks and roasted Jerusalem artichokes with the bacon broth and mashed potato.

Roast partridge with lentils, sausage and kale

Partridge is one of the earliest game birds you'll be able to buy during the game season, usually appearing at the start of September, and it's also my favourite. It has a naturally milder flavour and is sweeter and more tender than some of the meatier birds, such as pheasant and grouse, so often it is a good introduction for people who are new to game or are nervous of game meat tasting too strong. There's an impression that you need to hang game for a long time – it tenderises the meat – but in fact it's the hanging that also deepens the flavour, so I don't think that's necessary; I like mine quite fresh.

4 x oven-ready grey partridges (ask your butcher to prepare them for you)
100g butter, softened, plus extra for the kale
1 tbsp olive oil
4 good-quality pork sausages (about 280g total weight)
1 onion, finely diced
80g bacon lardons
½ carrot, finely diced
½ leek, washed and diced
1 garlic clove, crushed
1 celery stick, finely diced
¼ celeriac (about 200g), peeled and diced
175g puy lentils, rinsed and drained
300ml chicken bone broth
200g chestnut or girolle mushrooms
1½ tbsp chopped parsley
1½ tbsp chopped chives
500g kale, washed and tough stems removed
salt and pepper

Preheat the oven to 200°C/gas 6.

Rub the partridges with half the softened butter, season well and place in the oven. Roast for 25–30 minutes. Remove from the oven, cover with foil and leave to rest.

Meanwhile, melt the olive oil and a tablespoon of butter in a large frying pan over a medium heat and brown the sausages, then remove from the pan. Add the onion and lardons to the pan and cook for 2 minutes. Next add the carrot, leek, garlic, celery and celeriac and cook for a further 2 minutes. Add the lentils with 500ml water, the bone broth and browned sausages and season well with salt and pepper. Reduce the heat and simmer for 25–30 minutes.

Meanwhile, melt the remaining butter in a frying pan and fry the mushrooms until soft all the way through and browned. Once cooked, add to the cooked lentils with the parsley and chives and stir through.

Add the kale to a pan with just the water clinging to its leaves. Cover and cook over a medium heat until just wilted, about 3 minutes. Drain well and toss with a little butter.

Spoon the mushrooms, lentils and sausages into a serving dish, lay the partridges on the top and serve with the buttered kale.

Rice pudding with poached plums

Pudding is something I eat very rarely – I would much sooner get stuck into a cheeseboard if we're finishing a meal in a more elaborate way at home – but my husband has a very sweet tooth, and I will make a few exceptions, this rice pudding being one of them. It is something we'll often have at the end of a family meal after a bracing walk. There's something so warming and comforting in the soothing, simple flavour of a steaming bowl of rice pudding and it can be made as sweet as each person likes it. These lightly poached plums are a wonderful way to make use of the wild plums that are abundant in the hedgerows around Daylesford (though if you're serving this to children leave out the liqueur). You could stew any kind of seasonal berry, soft fruit or apple if you prefer, sweetening it to your taste.

100g short grain rice
1 vanilla pod, split lengthways, seeds scraped out
400ml full-fat milk
150ml double cream
50g caster sugar
50g mascarpone
small handful of toasted walnuts halves, to decorate

FOR THE PLUMS
1 vanilla pod, split lengthways
60g caster sugar
30ml plum liqueur
4 plums, halved and stones removed

Put the rice, vanilla seeds, milk, cream and sugar into a pan, place over a medium heat and slowly bring to the boil. Simmer for about 25–30 minutes, stirring occasionally, until thickened. Remove from the heat and allow to cool slightly before folding in the mascarpone. Leave to one side while you prepare the plums.

Put the vanilla pod, sugar and plum liqueur into a pan with 150ml water and place over a medium heat. Heat gently until the sugar is dissolved, then add the plums and poach for about 10 minutes. Keep a close eye: you want the plums to soften, but also to keep their shape. Transfer the plums to a bowl and then reduce the poaching liquid until it thickens a little. Pour this over the plums.

To serve, place a generous spoonful of rice pudding into a bowl, then top with two plum halves and a drizzle of the reduced poaching liquid. Decorate with a few walnuts and serve.

AUTUMN • SERVES 10–12

Honey parfait with poached pears, honeycomb and lemon curd

This pudding was inspired by my love of the bees and is a celebration of their work. Supporting Britain's bees is something I am incredibly passionate about. As pollinators, bees are vital in ensuring that future generations are able to live off the land as we can, so having plenty of honey in our hives is a sign that our bees are collecting nectar and thriving. The pudding requires a little more time than some of the other recipes in the book if you are going to make every element, but you could always make the parfait alone and serve it with some good-quality lemon curd.

FOR THE PARFAIT
75g heather honey (or other floral runny honey)
25g caster sugar
4 medium egg yolks
1 tbsp lemon juice
250ml whipping cream
25g bee pollen

FOR THE POACHED PEARS
500g caster sugar
2 vanilla pods, split lengthways
6 pears, peeled, halved and cored

FOR THE HONEYCOMB
200g caster sugar
2 tbsp heather honey (or other floral runny honey)
3 tbsp golden syrup
2 tsp bicarbonate of soda

FOR THE LEMON CURD
zest and juice of 4 lemons
200g caster sugar
3 medium eggs
2 medium egg yolks
100g unsalted butter, cubed

To make the parfait, line a terrine or loaf tin, approximately 23 x 9 x 8cm, with cling film, leaving some overlapping the sides. Put the honey, caster sugar, egg yolks and lemon juice into a large heatproof bowl set over a pan of gently simmering water and whisk until frothy and thick, about 20 minutes. Remove the bowl from the heat and set aside to cool. Meanwhile use a hand-held electric whisk to whip the cream to soft peaks. Fold into the cooled mixture with the bee pollen and pour into the lined terrine tin. Fold the overhanging cling film over the top and transfer to the freezer.

To poach the pears make a syrup by putting 1 litre water into a large pan with the caster sugar and vanilla pods. Bring to the boil and then simmer for 3 minutes. Add the prepared pears and cover the pan. Poach gently for about 20 minutes; when they are cooked remove with a slotted spoon and leave to cool.

Next make the honeycomb. Line a baking tray with baking parchment. Put the caster sugar, honey and golden syrup into a large pan, bring to the boil and allow to bubble for about 10 minutes until lightly golden. Add the bicarbonate of soda – stand back as it will sizzle. Pour onto the lined tray and leave to set until hard enough to snap, about 1–1½ hours.

To make the lemon curd, put all the ingredients into a large heatproof bowl set over a pan of simmering water. Stir until the sugar is dissolved and then continue to heat gently for about 20 minutes, until thick enough to coat the back of a spoon. Strain through a fine-mesh sieve and, if not using immediately, pour into a warm sterilised jar (see page 201). Keep in the fridge once cool.

Remove the parfait from the freezer about 10 minutes before serving. Turn out and slice, then serve with a poached pear half, a spoon of lemon curd and some shards of honeycomb.

BLACKBERRIES, SLOES AND HEDGEROW FRUITS

SEPTEMBER–NOVEMBER

The hedgerows and woodlands are a plentiful autumn larder and for me the blackberries, wild plums, damsons and sloes they offer are some of the great joys of the season, not simply for their flavour and versatility but also because a forage among the brambles is something I never tire of doing.

I always took my children blackberrying with me when they were young, and now I love watching my grandchildren's faces light up as they scramble among the hedgerows. Picking berries – be that in the summer at a pick-your-own farm or with an autumn rummage in the woods – can be one of the first ways children really engage with where their food comes from so foraging is something I want to see continue. It was an activity that was in danger of being lost in the 1970s when so many British hedgerows were ripped out, but now that they are slowly returning, the hedgerows can provide a free and sustainable source of food, provided we respect them and collect responsibly. Wild food is very important for the survival of the UK's wildlife so we need to forage with care to ensure there is enough left for birds and others, and to allow the plants to reproduce.

Blackberries should be available wherever you are in the country: they pop up in riverbanks, parks and hedgerows in towns and in the countryside – though I wouldn't suggest picking the berries from busy roads because of the pollution, nor any that are low down.

Sloes aren't so common in an urban setting, but go to the countryside and you'll spot the bushes. A blackthorn shrub in full fruit is a beautiful thing; the blueish-black sloe berries huddled in dense clusters around the branches. There's lots of debate around when to pick sloes – some believe you need to wait until after the first frost, but I simply pick mine when I can squash the fruits between my fingers easily.

We'll always get straight into the kitchen to put our foraged haul to use: either preserved as pots of blackberry or hedgerow jam and jellies, or baked in one of my favourite puddings – blackberry and apple pie. Making sloe gin and damson vodka is another annual tradition. I'll always let the berries steep for a year as I think they're best when left that long so it's an exciting moment when we open the previous year's bottle – usually to mark the start of the festive season.

WOOTTON
NOVEMBER

Wootton is our family farm up in Staffordshire and it was here that we first made the switch to organic farming. The estate is at the bottom of the Peak District so the land is wilder and more rugged than at Daylesford. The ground undulates and the landscape changes dramatically as you cross the estate, from the grassland across the hills where the sheep graze to the woodland, with its heavy coverage of leafy oaks and thick undergrowth.

Wootton really comes into its own in the autumn when the trees are like a tapestry of greens, browns and ochres. They change so quickly and each morning as I step out into the park to walk the dogs I always wonder what I am going to find. As the season progresses, the leaves turn deep violet and aubergine and by the winter the woods are almost a purple haze. The views from the hills are breathtaking – it feels like the Staffordshire countryside is laid out before you, unobstructed by roads or vehicles.

Staffordshire is sheep country. It's not very good arable land but we do have a lot of sheep. We also rear our herd of beef cattle – Aberdeen Angus – which are hardier than our dairy cows and thrive in the cold weather. We also have table chickens and a wonderful herd of deer, the largest herd of organically farmed deer in the country.

My husband's father bought the estate when there were four deer parks. When he took it over the deer were wild but when we became organic we tagged them and began a breeding programme.

Wootton's wild landscapes and rolling hills draw me into nature whatever the weather.

Our red deer are much closer to wild animals in their behaviour than any of our other livestock and this of course affects how they live and how they are treated. They roam and graze hundreds of acres of parkland and as far as is possible within a farmed context they live as they would as wild animals. The deer are tended to by just two stockmen, who have a deep knowledge and understanding of their characteristics and how they behave. The hinds give birth unassisted and the calves are left with their mothers until they are weaned just before

Christmas. And because the Staffordshire winters can be frosty, we house most of the hinds and calves over the winter.

Caring for our animals is our biggest priority and we want to ensure that the end of their lives is as peaceful and stress-free as possible. It is for this reason that we built our own abattoir at Wootton. The animals are settled for at least a day in the fields before going into the deep straw-bed barn of the abattoir (known as 'lairage'), where they settle further before being walked into the abattoir. They're not cattle-trucked to somewhere where they are frightened, and there is a vet present at all times. It is as peaceful and humane a process as is possible.

Oxtail stew with mash and cabbage

The food I eat in autumn and winter is often about nourishing my body with the goodness that comes from cooking very slowly and simply, and nurturing my soul with the comfort of tucking into a warming plate. Slow-cooking the cheap cuts is something my mother used to do every week when I was a child so there's also a lot of nostalgia wrapped up in this recipe, but I still believe cheap cuts like oxtail and beef cheeks are the tastiest. The meat has been slowly broken down to become so tender, and alongside the gentle bite of the root vegetables and cabbage and creamy mash this is my idea of heaven.

1.5kg oxtail
2–3 tbsp seasoned flour
2–3 tbsp olive oil
2 carrots, sliced
1 celery stick, sliced
2 onions, sliced
6 garlic cloves, sliced
500ml red wine
1.5 litres beef bone broth
6 sprigs of thyme
salt and pepper

FOR THE MASHED POTATO
500g floury potatoes, peeled and halved
60ml double cream
75g unsalted butter, softened

FOR THE CABBAGE
250g bacon lardons
1 garlic clove, crushed
2 carrots, diced
150g celeriac, peeled and diced
150g swede, peeled and diced
1 small savoy cabbage, shredded

Preheat the oven to 150°C/gas 2.

Dust the oxtail with the seasoned flour. Heat the olive oil in a large, heavy-based casserole dish and sear the oxtail until browned and then remove from the pan – this is best done in batches. Add the carrots, celery, onions and garlic to the pan and soften for about 10–15 minutes.

Add the red wine and simmer until reduced a little, then add the broth and thyme sprigs and season with salt and pepper. Add the browned oxtail, bring back to the boil and then transfer to the oven for about 3 hours, removing the lid for the last hour. The oxtail meat should come away from the bone easily.

Towards the end of the cooking time, cook the potatoes in boiling salted water until soft, about 15–20 minutes. Drain and mash until smooth, then beat in the cream and butter.

Meanwhile, fry the bacon lardons in a pan until they release some of their fat, then add the garlic, carrots, celeriac and swede. Cook over a low heat with a lid on until the vegetables are soft, about 10–15 minutes. Add the shredded cabbage to the pan, replace the lid and cook for a further 5–10 minutes. Season and serve with the oxtail and mashed potato.

WINTER

FROM THE
MARKET GARDEN

DECEMBER
Brussels sprouts
cavolo nero
jerusalem artichokes
leeks
parsnips
potatoes
red cabbage
savoy cabbage
shallots
swede
squash
turnip

JANUARY
Brussels sprouts
celeriac
january king cabbage
jerusalem artichokes
kale
leeks
parsnips
rosemary
swede
thyme
turnip

FEBRUARY
chervil
endive
jerusalem artichokes
kale
leeks
parsnips
sprouting broccoli
savoy cabbage
salsify
winter purslane

As the rusty, burnished tones of the autumn give way to simple white buds, green and silver branches, and bright festive berries, I know that winter has arrived. But though the garden is in bloom, much of the landscape at the farm is bare and bleak; the tops of the leeks and the bold, brave brassicas – kales, cabbages, Brussels sprouts and broccoli – the only visible reminders that there is still life in the soil. The thick layer of mist or the dusting of frost on the leaves might look menacing, but it is this first snap of cold that is thought to improve the flavour of the vegetables. It brings out a natural sweetness in them and signifies that now is a good time to harvest.

All the winter greens are wonderful, each with its own unique iron-rich flavour, but I am particularly fond of the humble Brussels sprout. And although they can be cut from their stalks well before the winter I do think sprouts taste better with a little frost on them. As does celery. Celery can be a very underrated, even unpopular vegetable but I love its peppery crunch; it's so delicious with blue cheese and walnuts, and I love using the tops in a soup or to top a winter salad.

And of course the game season is well under way. My favourite is partridge – roasted with the last of the autumn's blackberries or damsons, or on top of a hearty lentil base – but we have several wild birds come to the farm: pheasant, teal, snipe and grouse. And up at Wootton we have our venison. I know many people are quite nervous of venison's flavour, describing it as overly 'gamey', and while I agree that wild venison can have quite a strong flavour, the lifestyle and habitat of our farmed deer (see page 219) means that its taste is milder; and it is very tender. Venison is often cooked slowly, in stews, to mask its flavour or to make it less tough, but our venison is so tender I love it cooked very quickly; the leanness of the meat means that's all it needs (see page 240 for our Venison ragu with pappardelle).

It's easy to forget that cheeses are seasonal but artisan cheeses do have their seasons depending on what the cows, sheep or goats are eating throughout the year. I'll always try to include a seasonal choice on my cheeseboards when I can. Mont d'Or is a particularly special experience at this time of year – housed in a spruce wooden box, it is a creamy, tangy, earthy and decadent cheese with a strong smell, which you either adore or find very overpowering. When it's perfectly ripe, Mont d'Or can just be spooned out of its container, but it can also be baked until golden and bubbling. It's a wonderful treat and something I love to indulge in at this time of year. Christmas and Cheddar are also heavily intertwined for me because by Christmastime our Cheddar will have aged in our creamery for 18 months and is at the peak of its flavour.

The colours at this time of year are rusty and muted and I'll try and celebrate that change when I'm laying a table through what I forage from the garden for decoration. The turning of the leaves brings a new palette and it's so easy to decorate a table or mark place settings just with dried leaves.

WINTER • SERVES 4

Jerusalem artichoke soup

Even for gardeners who are new to tending a vegetable patch, Jerusalem artichokes are relatively easy to grow. We will inevitably have an abundance at the farm so they're something I eat a lot over the winter months in various forms. Yet Jerusalem artichokes are not loved. Perhaps it's their knobbly shape and the fact that they can be tricky to peel, but while parsnips and squash will be snapped up at the farm shops, some of our customers need a little more persuasion where Jerusalem artichokes are concerned. In this soup, their sweet, nutty flesh is blended down into a wonderfully thick and velvety texture and I'm hoping it might convert some sceptics. The artichoke crisps are very quick and easy to prepare and if you double or treble the batch, they're also a lovely thing to serve with drinks as a nibble.

2 tbsp olive oil
35g unsalted butter
1 large onion, finely chopped
1 garlic clove, chopped
1 large sprig of thyme, leaves picked
1kg Jerusalem artichokes, peeled and roughly chopped
750ml vegetable stock

250ml full-fat milk
90ml double cream
salt and pepper

TO GARNISH
2 Jerusalem artichokes, unpeeled
50g butter, cut into small cubes

Preheat the oven to 180°C/gas 4.

Melt the olive oil and butter together in a large pan over a medium heat. Add the onion, garlic and thyme leaves and soften until sticky and aromatic, making sure that the mixture doesn't catch.

Add the artichokes to the pan, and cook until just tender when pierced with a knife. Cover with the stock and simmer for about 20 minutes until soft.

Meanwhile, prepare the garnish. Cut the 2 artichokes in half, dot with butter and place on a baking tray. Roast for about 30 minutes until golden and crispy. Remove and set aside.

Add the milk and cream to the soup and cook for a further 2 minutes before liquidising with a hand-held stick blender. Season to taste with salt and pepper.

Serve the warm soup in bowls, with the roasted artichokes on the side.

WINTER • SERVES 6

Onion and cider soup with rarebit

Aside from providing inspiration for chutneys (see page 201), the farm's plentiful supply of apples also enables us to make our own cider and Jez, our head gardener at Daylesford, is a particularly keen cider-brewer. This soup was inspired by our heritage apple orchard (for more about the orchard see page 198). I think it's clear by now that I cannot resist cheese but melted cheese holds a special place in my heart. In my opinion, what wintry supper is not improved when served with some tangy, melting cheese on toast?

2 tbsp light olive oil
500g onions, thinly sliced
1 garlic clove, crushed
150ml Madeira
150ml medium dry cider
1.5 litres beef bone broth
small bunch of thyme, leaves picked
pinch of paprika, per serving
salt and pepper

FOR THE RAREBIT
350g Cheddar, grated
80ml milk
25g plain flour
20g English mustard
10ml Worcestershire sauce
1 medium egg, plus 1 egg yolk
6 slices of sourdough bread

Place a large pan over a medium heat and add the olive oil. Sweat the onions with a little salt for about 15 minutes until soft and golden, then add the garlic.

Pour in the Madeira and cider to deglaze the pan, and cook until the liquid has almost evaporated before adding the beef broth. Bring to the boil slowly, then lower the heat and simmer for 45 minutes, then check the seasoning.

Meanwhile, prepare the rarebit. Put the cheese and milk in a pan and melt slowly over a medium heat, stirring to make sure the mixture does not catch. Add the flour, mustard and Worcestershire sauce and mix thoroughly, then take off the heat and leave to cool. When the mixture has cooled sufficiently so as to prevent the egg from cooking, beat in the whole egg and yolk.

When you are nearly ready to serve, preheat the oven to 180°C/gas 4. Spread the rarebit mixture over the sourdough slices, place on a baking tray and put in the oven for 8–10 minutes, or until golden brown on top and slightly crispy underneath. Cut each slice in half.

Serve the soup in bowls with a few thyme leaves, a sprinkling of paprika and the rarebit on the side.

Winter greens

When I go to California to visit my daughter Alice, we will eat a chopped salad almost every day. They're something I think the Americans have mastered perfectly and this recipe was simply a way of recreating their idea at home, shining the spotlight on the farm's abundance of seasonal greens. I think a chopped salad should be well dressed, but adjust the quantity to your taste.

150g courgettes, finely diced
½ broccoli (about 200g), florets sliced on a mandolin
½ cauliflower (about 200g), florets sliced on a mandolin
40g kale, stalks removed and leaves finely chopped
60g white cabbage, sliced on a mandolin
½ cucumber, deseeded and finely diced
4 spring onions, finely chopped
1½ tbsp chervil leaves

1½ tbsp parsley leaves
1½ tbsp mint leaves
125ml olive oil
25ml avocado oil
50g Dijon mustard
50ml cider vinegar
salt and pepper

Mix all the prepared vegetables and herbs together in a serving dish.

Whisk together the oils, mustard and cider vinegar and season to taste with salt and pepper. Gently fold the dressing through the salad and serve.

WINTER • SERVES 4

Flat-iron chicken and kale

This light dish, full of lean protein and nourishing nutrients, is one we try to keep on the menu at Daylesford's cafés for as long as we have kale. Crunchy thanks to the nuts with a hint of natural sweetness from the apples and dressing, it also happens to be one of my favourites.

4 x chicken breasts (about 160g each)
3 garlic cloves, crushed
40ml olive oil
juice of ½ lemon
salt and pepper

FOR THE SALAD
120g pecans, broken into bite-sized pieces
3 tbsp caster sugar
small pinch of cayenne pepper
40ml white wine vinegar
50ml olive oil
1 tbsp wholegrain mustard
2 tbsp clear honey
250g kale, stalks removed and leaves roughly chopped
2 apples, unpeeled, cored and cut into batons

Lay the chicken breasts between sheets of cling film and gently flatten using a meat tenderiser or rolling pin. Put the chicken into a dish and rub with the garlic and olive oil, then season with salt and pepper. Cover and leave in the fridge to marinate for as long as possible (ideally overnight). Remove the chicken from the fridge and bring to room temperature before cooking.

Preheat the oven to 180°C/gas 4.

Soak the pecans in warm water for 10–15 minutes, then drain and pat dry with kitchen paper. Mix together the sugar, cayenne pepper and a pinch of salt in a small bowl and toss in the dried pecans. Place the nuts on a small baking tray lined with baking parchment and bake in the oven until the sugar is lightly caramelised and the pecans are golden, about 5–10 minutes, then leave to cool.

Preheat a ridged griddle pan and cook the flattened chicken breasts for about 5 minutes each side until cooked. Squeeze over the lemon juice and leave to rest while you assemble the salad.

Whisk together the vinegar, olive oil, mustard and honey and check for seasoning. Toss the kale with the dressing and then mix in the apple batons and candied pecans. Serve with the rested chicken breasts.

WINTER • SERVES 4

Bone marrow and barley risotto

One of the pillars of our sustainability programme at Daylesford is to try and reduce our waste, which includes trying to avoid food waste. I grew up in a time when as little as possible was thrown away and that philosophy has stayed with me. When an animal was slaughtered, as much of it was sold as possible, so my mother regularly bought offal; in part because it was cheaper but also because it enhanced the flavour of our food. I know offal is not to everyone's taste but it is something that I still enjoy and if an animal is to be killed I want to respect that. If you'd like to consider trying to eat more offal, this risotto might encourage you. Bone marrow is used to add richness and enhance flavour and here it is mellowed by mixing it with butter.

260g pearl barley
60g cavolo nero leaves
600ml beef bone broth
60g Parmesan, grated
1 tbsp chopped parsley
salt and pepper

FOR THE BONE MARROW BUTTER
350g bone marrow
125g unsalted butter, at room temperature
1 tsp truffle oil
1 tbsp Marmite (or other yeast extract)
1 shallot, diced
1 garlic clove, crushed
1 tbsp finely chopped parsley

FOR THE SEED MIX
70g sunflower seeds
55g cashew nuts
50g hazelnuts
50g walnuts
50g pumpkin seeds
50g linseeds
90g oats
3 tbsp soy sauce
1 garlic clove, grated
pinch of paprika

First make the bone marrow butter. Preheat the oven to 120°C/gas ½. Put the bone marrow on a baking tray and roast for 10 minutes to loosen the marrow. Once cooked, scoop the marrow out into a heatproof bowl and set aside. Meanwhile combine the butter, truffle oil and Marmite in a separate bowl.

Add the shallots and garlic to the bowl of bone marrow and then place over a pan of simmering water for a couple of minutes, just until the marrow starts to soften. Add this to the butter along with the parsley and mix well. Put into the fridge for 2–3 minutes, then when it starts to firm up, turn out on to a piece of cling film and roll into a log, wrapping it tightly. Chill until needed. Leftover butter can be stored in the fridge for a week or frozen for a month.

Now prepare the seed mix. Increase the oven temperature to 160°C/gas 3 and line a baking tray with baking parchment. Mix together all the ingredients, spread out on the lined tray and leave for 15–20 minutes before transferring to the oven for 10–12 minutes, or until golden. Remove from the oven and cool, then gently grind in a pestle and mortar or with a rolling pin.

Bring a large pan of water to the boil and add the barley. Cook, following the instructions on the packet, then drain and leave to cool. Bring a medium pan of water to the boil and add the cavolo nero. Blanch for 2–3 minutes, then drain and refresh under cold water. Roughly chop and leave to one side. Bring 400ml of the stock to the boil in a wide pan. Reduce to a simmer and add the cooked barley and seed mix and cook for 2–3 minutes, stirring. Add 200g of the bone marrow butter (you can keep the rest in the fridge) and continue to cook, gradually adding more beef stock until you have a risotto-like consistency, about 5 minutes. Season to taste, then add the cavolo nero, grated Parmesan and parsley and stir until warmed through.

WINTER • SERVES 4

Venison ragu with pappardelle

Venison can be cooked two ways – either very quickly, just to sear it, or slowly braised. The venison we farm up at Wootton is very lean so it is well suited to being quickly fried. However, because there's no fat on it, it's easy to overcook the meat. If you're worried about overcooking yours, then this simple sauce is a perfect introduction to it. The sauce is also delicious served on a jacket potato.

1.1kg venison haunch, trimmed and diced
    (ask your butcher to do this for you)
185ml red wine
olive oil, for frying
50g streaky bacon lardons
2 tbsp tomato purée
2 sprigs of thyme
2 tbsp flour

1.2 litres chicken bone broth
400g dried pappardelle pasta
400g assorted mushrooms, sliced (our chefs suggest a seasonal combination such as Portobello, chestnut and girolle)
4 tbsp chopped parsley
60g finely grated Parmesan
salt and pepper

A day or two before you want to make the ragu, place the venison in a large, flat-bottomed dish, pour over the wine, cover and leave to marinate in the fridge for at least 24 hours, and up to 48 hours, turning the meat over a couple of times during this time.

When you are ready to cook, preheat the oven to 165°C/gas 3½. Drain the venison, reserving the marinade, and pat the meat dry with kitchen paper.

In a pan over a medium heat, heat a little olive oil and fry the venison in batches until browned all over, then use a slotted spoon to transfer to a lidded casserole dish.

Using the same frying pan, fry the lardons until starting to crisp, then add the tomato purée, thyme sprigs and flour. Cook for 2 minutes, then slowly add the marinade liquid a little at a time, allowing the mixture to thicken and reduce before adding a little more. Once fully combined, gradually add the broth, stirring to avoid any lumps. Bring to a simmer and then pour the mixture over the venison. Cover with a lid and cook for about 2½ hours, or until the venison is tender. Season to taste.

Cook the pappardelle in lightly salted boiling water for 8–9 minutes, or according to the packet instructions, then drain well.

While the pasta is cooking, sauté the mushrooms over a medium heat in a little oil. Add them to the venison ragu. Gently stir in the cooked pasta and chopped parsley and scatter with the grated Parmesan. Serve immediately.

WINTER • SERVES 4

Slow-cooked pigs' cheeks with turnip, apple, hazelnuts and celeriac mash

Cheeks are another cut that need very long, slow cooking. Pigs do a lot of chewing so it follows that the cheek is a very muscular cut and that muscle needs time to be broken down until it becomes tender. Patience is definitely a virtue here: the result of the hours that you leave it in the oven is meat that is so soft you could eat it with a spoon, and a delicious rich gravy that is crying out for a loose buttery mash to soak it all up. Eating is all about balance for me; there's simply no question over mash — it needs lots of cream and butter.

2 tbsp olive oil, plus extra for drizzling
8 pigs' cheeks, trimmed
6 onions, 2 of them sliced, 4 of them cut in half horizontally
1 carrot, chopped
2 celery sticks, chopped
2 garlic cloves, sliced
250ml white wine
600ml pork bone broth or light chicken stock
12 baby turnips, peeled and thinly sliced
8 cavolo nero leaves
1 apple, unpeeled, cored and cut into batons
25g toasted hazelnuts, roughly chopped
salt and pepper

FOR THE CELERIAC MASH
1 medium celeriac, peeled and chopped
100g butter
100ml double cream

Preheat the oven to 150°C/gas 2.

Heat the olive oil in a large lidded ovenproof dish and brown the cheeks all over, in batches. Remove from the pan and set aside. Add the sliced onions, carrot, celery and garlic to the pan and cook gently for about 5 minutes, stirring. Return the pigs' cheeks to the pan, add the wine and reduce by half. Add the broth and season with salt and pepper, then cover with the lid and cook in the oven for 3 hours, removing the lid for the last half hour.

Drizzle the remaining onions with a little olive oil, place in a dish and roast in the oven with the pig cheeks for about 45 minutes. Push the outer layers out to make little cups.

When you are nearly ready to serve, bring a large pan of water to the boil and cook the baby turnips for 12–15 minutes, or until tender.

Prepare the celeriac mash: cook the celeriac in boiling water until soft. Drain well and mash well (or use a potato ricer) with the butter and cream, adding seasoning to taste.

Bring a pan of salted water to the boil and blanch the cavolo nero leaves for 2–3 minutes. Drain and quickly refresh in cold water, then roughly chop.

Serve the pigs' cheeks, with the celeriac mash, onion cups, baby turnips and cavolo nero leaves, garnished with the apple batons and chopped hazelnuts.

WINTER • SERVES 4

Beef shin stew with Marmite and Cheddar dumplings

Shin is the meat to choose for stews in my opinion. Like other cuts on the bone, the shin is packed full of deep flavour, yet the meat collapses to become silky. There are few things more welcoming or bolstering on a cold winter's day than a pot of stew, but a stew bobbing with cheesy dumplings is perfection. If you're not a Marmite lover as I am you can leave it out, but I do think it gives the dumplings a lovely savoury tang that is perfect against the richness of the meat liquor.

2 tbsp olive oil
1kg beef shin (bone in)
1 carrot, diced
1 celery stick, diced
2 garlic cloves, crushed
300ml Madeira
1.5 litres beef bone broth
2 sprigs of rosemary
salt and pepper

FOR THE DUMPLINGS
50g suet
30g Cheddar, grated
100g self-raising flour, plus extra for dusting
25g Marmite (or other yeast extract)

FOR THE GARNISH
3 carrots, cut into batons
3 onions, cut into wedges
olive oil, for drizzling
large handful of cavolo nero (about 16 leaves)
3 cooked beetroot, peeled and diced
2cm piece of fresh horseradish, peeled and grated
handful of snipped chives

Preheat the oven to 150°C/gas 2. Put a large pan or casserole with a lid over a medium heat and add the olive oil, then brown the beef until golden all over. Remove the beef from the pan and cover with foil.

Return the pan to the heat, add the carrot, celery and garlic and cook for a few minutes until softened. Pour in the Madeira to deglaze the pan, stirring to scrape up any browned bits from the base of the pan. Let it bubble for a minute or two, then strain to remove and discard the vegetables. Return the beef to the pan with the strained Madeira. Add the stock and rosemary sprigs, and season with salt and pepper. Cover and put into the oven for 4½ hours. After 3½ hours, put the carrots and onions for the garnish into a roasting tray, drizzle with olive oil and season. Roast in the oven for the remaining hour.

Meanwhile, get on with the dumplings. In a large mixing bowl, combine the suet, Cheddar, flour, yeast extract and a little salt. Gradually add 4–5 tablespoons of cold water until the mixture binds together to form a dough. Flour your hands to prevent the mixture sticking, and roll into eight balls, about 25g each. Thirty minutes before the end of the stew's cooking time, mix half the dumplings into the stew and sit the other half on top of it, then cover the pan and return to the oven.

Next, prepare the cavolo nero. Bring a pan of water to the boil and add the cavolo nero. Blanch for 2–3 minutes, then drain and refresh under cold water. Roughly chop and leave to one side.

Remove the stew and roast vegetables from the oven; the dumplings on top should be golden, and the onions and carrots soft and sweet. Carefully transfer to a serving dish, making sure to spread out the dumplings, or serve in the casserole dish itself. Garnish with the roasted carrots and onions, cavolo nero and diced beetroot. Sprinkle grated horseradish and chives on the top to finish.

WINTER • SERVES 8–10

Egg custard tart with clementines, ginger and pecans

Although you can find plenty of wonderful varieties of custard tart around the world, I have to confess a preference for the very traditional British version. I like the custard to be quite firm and not too sweet, and the tart has to be baked in a deep tin so that it's a generous layer. The pastry should be crisp and biscuity and I love the warmth of nutmeg so ours is always finished with a heavy dusting of the spice.

FOR THE PASTRY
450g plain flour
280g unsalted butter, diced
3 medium eggs
100g icing sugar
1 vanilla pod, split lengthways and seeds scraped out

FOR THE FILLING
500ml double cream
500ml full-fat milk
340g caster sugar
16 medium egg yolks
grated nutmeg

TO SERVE
5 clementines, peeled, pith removed and segmented
100g raisins
300g caster sugar
300ml water
100g crystallised ginger, diced
75g pecans, halved

Tip the flour into a bowl, add the diced butter and rub in with your fingertips until the mixture resembles breadcrumbs. Lightly beat 2 of the eggs and add to the bowl along with the icing sugar and vanilla seeds and mix until you have a dough. When it has come together into a ball, wrap in cling film and leave to chill in the fridge for at least 30 minutes.

Roll the pastry out on a floured surface to a thickness of about 3mm and use to line a straight-sided tart tin, 24cm in diameter and 7cm deep. Trim away the excess pastry and lightly prick the base with a fork. Chill in the fridge for another 30 minutes. Preheat the oven to 170°C/gas 3.

Line the base of the tart with baking parchment, fill with baking beans and bake blind for 30 minutes until the pastry browns lightly, removing the paper and beans for the last 10 minutes. Beat the remaining egg and use to brush over the base, then pop back in the oven for another 2–3 minutes. Remove from the oven and set aside while you make the filling. Reduce the oven temperature to 140°C/gas 1.

In a large bowl whisk together the cream, milk, caster sugar and egg yolks. Place the tart tin on a baking tray and pour in the custard. Grate over a little nutmeg and carefully transfer to the oven to bake for about 1 hour, or until the custard has set but still has a slight wobble in the centre.

Put the prepared clementines and raisins into a bowl. Put the sugar into a pan with 300ml water and bring to the boil, swirling gently until the sugar has completely dissolved. Pour over the clementines and raisins and leave to cool. Gently stir in the ginger and pecans and serve with the custard tart.

WINTER • SERVES 8

Steamed ginger pudding

This pudding reminds me of time spent with my family in Wootton; of wintry walks in the frosty woods, log fires and long Sunday lunches. Sticky, sweet and reviving, this pudding is made for those days — best lingered over with a strong coffee or revitalising cup of tea.

1 x 454g tin golden syrup
570ml full-fat milk
225g fresh white breadcrumbs
225g plain flour
225g suet
2 tbsp bicarbonate of soda
2 medium eggs, beaten

1 x 350g jar preserved stem ginger, drained and chopped
1 tsp ground ginger
1 tsp mixed spice
2 tsp baking powder
pinch of salt
Poached Rhubarb (see page 146), to serve (optional)
custard, cream or ice cream, to serve

Grease a 1.2 litre pudding basin and line the base with a circle of baking parchment. Spoon a little of the golden syrup over the base.

In a large pan over a low heat, heat the milk and syrup together until the syrup has melted. Remove from the heat and then mix in the breadcrumbs, flour, suet and bicarbonate of soda. Add the eggs, stem ginger, ground ginger, mixed spice, baking powder and salt. Fold together until combined – the mixture should be quite runny. Pour the mixture into the prepared pudding basin.

Cut two large squares of baking parchment or foil and make a wide pleat in the middle of each one. Lay them both over the top of the pudding basin – the pleats will allow room for the pudding to rise. Secure the paper or foil with string tied tightly around the rim of the pudding basin, leaving a length of string to make a handle so that the pudding can be lifted out of the pan easily.

Gently lower the basin into a large pan of boiling water – the water should come halfway up the basin. Cover and leave to steam for 2½ hours. You may need to top up with more boiling water – do not let the pan boil dry.

When the pudding is ready, very carefully lift the basin out of the pan. Cool a little then remove the foil or paper and loosen the edges of the pudding with a knife before turning out onto a large plate. Serve the pudding with the poached rhubarb, if you like, and custard, cream or ice cream.

CHRISTMAS
DECEMBER

It's hard not to get swept up in the sense of celebration and festivities that mark this time of year. I love the anticipation of Christmas, the preparations, both in the kitchen and in making the house look festive. And I love the feeling that things are slowing down; Christmas gives you the opportunity to spend more time with family and friends, and to reflect a little as the year draws to a close.

The kitchen is at the heart of so many Christmas traditions and my preparations begin back in October when I make our Christmas cake. But it's Stir-up Sunday when I really start to feel festive. My children and grandchildren will all come into the kitchen and we'll each take a turn at stirring the Christmas pudding mixture and making a wish. Even today I turn to the pudding recipe my mother taught me as a child. She always used to stir silver threepenny bits into our pudding and I still buy them on eBay so that I can do the same. With the pudding made and wrapped in its muslin, ready to be fed with brandy for the next few weeks, we'll open a bottle of our homemade sloe gin or damson vodka; advent begins and the anticipation of the following weeks sets in.

As a child, and later when I had my own children, decorating the house for Christmas was the moment when the festive season began and it is still something I look forward to every year. At Daylesford we work closely with women in developing communities in India to create handmade Christmas decorations. I first travelled to India in my twenties, drawn there like so many of my generation by a desire to discover yoga – and I fell in love with it. There's so much to learn in India. It is a very spiritual place and I have found a great deal of calm and peace through its teachings.

I have been very fortunate to have had the opportunity to go back to India time and again; it is a country that has influenced and enriched my life in so many ways that I've wanted to try and give something back to it. In 2001 my team and I set up a charitable trust to help people from some of the most disadvantaged communities in India access a better quality of life. A large proportion of the work that the Trust carries out is to provide literacy, skills and training. As part of that, we have set up training for women to learn traditional Indian handicraft skills, such as hand-looming, stitching and embroidery. The training enables mothers to stay close to their families while earning an income; they can be self-sufficient yet remain at the heart of their communities. Seeing their work and training come alive through the Christmas decorations we sell at the farm every year has been immensely moving and rewarding. and they are an important part of the festive array in my home.

A morning spent foraging in the hedgerows and woodland can produce an abundant harvest of berries, mistletoe and rich greenery – all perfect for winding into a beautiful festive wreath. We hold wreath-making classes on the farm come the end of November and it's something that's very easy to do at home (turn to page 256 for our guide to making your own).

I love Christmas carols. I love going to a traditional carol service and now that my children are no longer at school I'll always try to go to a service at one of the churches in London; the sense of reverence and solemnity in those big spaces always fills me with awe. I'd feel something was missing if I didn't go. And I'll always go and see my grandchildren's school nativity play, which I adore. It's these little things that make Christmas for me – they're simple things but they're traditions I continue to cherish.

On Christmas Eve, we'll always have a family dinner – something light, perhaps some smoked salmon, and then it's last-minute present wrapping. When my grandchildren are staying we'll leave out a carrot and some hay for Rudolph and sherry and a mince pie for Father Christmas; the stockings will be hung and then they'll be ushered upstairs.

While I do love big gatherings at Christmas and will very often have lots of people round for mulled wine on Christmas Eve, Christmas Day is a time for just our close family. We'll have breakfast and go to church together, and then we'll come home and open a few presents. There'll be Bloody Marys before lunch, followed by the Queen's speech. Lunch is also very traditional: always a turkey from the farm, with all the trimmings, stuffing at both ends, sausages wrapped in bacon; and then Christmas pudding, brandy butter, mince pies and rum sauce as well. We usually start with an egg dish – I'm not sure why, it's just one of those little rituals we have and nobody quite remembers how or why it started. There'll be crackers and jokes and paper hats. And after lunch we'll all go out to give the dogs a long walk before we settle down in front of a roaring fire to watch an old film – usually the same one every year.

Christmas is of course a time of much celebration and I adore that side of it, but the reason we mark Christmas, its true meaning and the reason behind the celebrations are also very important to me. It's a time for giving and above all it's a time to show gratitude for all that the year has given us. Throughout the year Daylesford works with a number of homeless shelters and charities as part of our endeavours to help tackle food poverty and minimise food waste, but Christmas is a time when we strive to give that little bit more. On Christmas Eve and again on New Year's Eve, we donate the unsold festive food and fresh produce from our farm shops to St Patrick's church in Soho, Le Passage in Pimlico and Emmaus in Gloucester to ensure that those without the means we have can be given hot food.

MAKING A WREATH

1 SOURCE OR CREATE YOUR BASE
At the farm we like to use a homemade willow frame for our wreaths using willow from our wetland coppice, but you can easily source ready-made wicker or wire frames. Working with a frame that's about the size of a dinner plate means you can easily get your hand through the centre as you're weaving the foliage around it. With wire frames we will often cover them in green moss, securing it in place with tying wire. It's an easy way to hide the wire and allows you to use very simple elements on top as the moss becomes a decorative element in itself.

2 COLLECT AND FORAGE
We like to forage what we can from around the farm but always start with lots of greenery. Box is a favourite shrub; we have a lot in the surrounding woodland and it's small-leafed and dense so it adds volume to a wreath. Norway spruce has a lovely dark green colour and a wonderful aroma, while the more unusual blue spruce offers a striking contrast in colour, as do small amounts of leylandii, which also has a wonderful smell; bay and of course lots of holly. For a gentle splash of colour, choose red crab apple, ilex and delicate white mistletoe. Once you have gathered everything you want, lay it all out in separate bundles or boxes.

3 BUNCH
Building your wreath using pre-tied bouquets of forage is the easiest method. Depending on the size of your wreath you will need 10–15 bunches. Choose a variety of greenery and coloured stems from each of your bundles and trim so that the stems are roughly the same length. Arrange these into posies and tie each one towards the base with string. The length and width of your posies will depend on how big you want your wreath to be.

4 WIRE AND WRAP
Lay the first posy on to the wreath at roughly a 45-degree angle. Using a reel of wire, secure on to the wreath with a few wraps of your tying wire, then tuck your second posy in tightly beside your first and wrap the wire round again. Using a reel of wire means that a single piece of wire will secure all the bouquets, rather than having lots of knots in the wreath. Wire rather than string also means that everything will be held very tightly. Repeat with your remaining posies until your wreath is completely covered and even.

HANG IT UP
Look at your wreath and decide in which direction you want it to hang. Tie a piece of string around the top and hang it inside or on your front door.

A Christmas table needs to feel warm and welcoming. My tables around Christmastime are all about the berries, holly and ivy or other finds foraged from the hedgerows; I love ivy strewn across the table. I like a bit of silver and red glass because they bring warmth as well and there are always plenty of candles.

WINTER • SERVES 4

Chestnut bubble and squeak

We have this bubble and squeak every year on Boxing Day, made of the previous day's leftovers and served hot out of the pan with cold cuts of turkey, ham or pheasant and some Piccalilli on the side (see page 202 for our recipe).

125g swede, peeled and cut into chunks
750g cold leftover mashed potatoes, or crushed boiled potatoes
2 tbsp olive oil
1 onion, sliced
2 garlic cloves, chopped
180g chestnuts (either fresh, cooked and peeled, or vacuum-packed), chopped
250–275g leftover cooked green veg (broccoli/cabbage/Brussels sprouts in any combination), chopped
2 tbsp chopped parsley
250g polenta
30g butter
salt and pepper

Cook the swede: put into a pan of cold water, bring to the boil and cook for about 5 minutes, until just soft. Drain well and then mash with the potatoes. Meanwhile, heat a tablespoon of the olive oil in a pan and fry the onion and garlic over a medium heat until softened but not coloured, about 5 minutes.

Put the mashed potato and swede into a large bowl and add the softened onion and garlic, chopped chestnuts, leftover green vegetables and parsley; season well with salt and pepper. Divide the mixture evenly into 8 and shape into 'cakes' approximately 125g each (you can also make one large cake). Preheat the oven to 180°C/gas 4.

Spread the polenta out on a plate and dust the cakes with it, pressing them gently into the polenta to form a crust. Heat the remaining olive oil and butter in a large frying pan and pan-fry the cakes over a medium heat for about 4–5 minutes each side, or until crisp and golden. Remove from the pan and transfer to a baking tray. Bake in the oven until hot all the way through, about 30 minutes.

TIME TO REFLECT
JANUARY

After the excitement of Christmas there's a pause: those days of calm between the rush and revelry of the big day and the bustle and build-up to New Year's Eve.

The first month of the new year is a period of reflection for me and that begins in those quiet days after Christmas when I can truly take time for myself, think about the past year and look to the one ahead. A new year is a time to be thankful for what I've had over the year, but for me it's also a time to start thinking of little things I can change next year.

On New Year's Eve, I make and write down my resolutions for the year – things I'd like to improve about myself; things I'd like to do. To my regret and my husband's amusement, 'learn French' is an annual feature but I'm hopeful that one day I will finally be able to cross it off the list.

And as I look to January I start to think about my wellness and especially my well-being: whether I'm feeling happy and comfortable in myself. That starts with slowing everything down and making things simple again. After the riches of the previous month, I do feel a need to return to simple foods: soothing, gentle soups; simply-cooked vegetables; nourishing, sustaining beans and lentils; and I turn to cleansing ingredients – ginger and fennel and lots of herbal teas. I don't want to start the year paying penance for any indulgences over the festivities – December is a wonderful time to share and enjoy indulgent food with others and I cherish that time, so January isn't a time for guilt. On the contrary, the start of the new month and year are my opportunity to bring back balance, to look inward and focus on nurturing myself. To nourish my body with the kinds of food it is naturally calling for, and give my mind time and space to relax and let go. It's a time to be kind to myself.

WELL-BEING

WELL-BEING

Well-being is a word that is not always fully understood, but for me it simply means being healthy and happy in body, mind and spirit. How we achieve well-being is personal to each of us so the section that follows is simply a guide to some of the means by which I try and nurture these three pillars in my life, and how at the farm we try and help provide guidance and assistance for others. Eating whole, organic foods is of course the foundation of a healthy body. It is the foundation on which I believe we should build and nurture our physical health, but, as you will learn in these pages, since my twenties I have also been fascinated by rituals and practices that help me achieve that same balance and nourishment in my mind and in my spirit.

I think of my well-being as holistic and the three pillars need to work together. There are of course times when we might need a little extra nurturing so this section also includes a few recipes that are designed to contain vitamins, minerals and nutrients to see us through times when our bodies might be feeling under stress. Above all I hope that these pages will inspire you to take time to nurture and care for yourself.

TIME TO BE STILL

I have practised yoga and meditation since I was young and they continue to help me nurture my own well-being every day. When you practise yoga or meditate you're creating your own space, a place and a time for yourself in your mind, bringing your awareness back to yourself.

Yoga and meditation concentrate my mind but above all they ground me and they look after my spirit. If I have to miss my practice for a few days I can feel it; I feel as though I'm off balance.

As part of my morning practice I meditate. When I practise with Vettri, my teacher, we will say a Sanskrit prayer together, reminding ourselves to be grateful for the day.

Yoga and meditation are not for everybody but they are practices I've come to believe in very deeply, for what I feel are the powerful effects they have on our health, mental and physical. For anybody looking to try and introduce just a few minutes of calm or self-contemplation into their day, below is a very simple guide for a technique I have found useful.

Find a comfortable seated pose with your spine in a neutral position.

Inhale slowly, allowing your lungs to expand without any strain. Inhale a little more, allowing the abdomen to expand. The whole process should be one continuous movement. There should be no force or unnecessary strain.

Now start to exhale slowly. Try to empty your lungs as much as possible without any strain by pulling the abdominal wall as near as possible to the spine. This completes one sequence. Practise five to ten cycles for a few weeks, slowly increasing the time up to ten minutes. Better still, be curious: seek out a yoga or meditation teacher and perhaps give a class a try.

TIME TO SLEEP

I know it's been said many times but good sleep really is one of the most fundamental and important pillars of wellness. Promoting good, restful sleep is something we have always encouraged at our Haybarn Spa and it has inspired many of the products we design at Bamford. I have always been very careful to try and get a good night's sleep whenever I can. Travel has made me particularly conscious of my sleep patterns and how important it is to be mindful of them in order to feel well.

Sleep is restorative – it's your body's time to repair itself. To have a good night's sleep it's important to respect your body's natural rhythms. Going to bed at the same time every night helps respect these rhythms, as does having a relaxing routine before bed so that your body and mind are rested and in a peaceful state, ready for sleep. I remove anything from my bedroom that stimulates my mind – my phone or tablet – and I take care to make sure my sleeping environment is gentle and calming: the lighting is low, and I have soft, natural bed linens to make my skin feel nurtured and comfortable. I'll often have a bath before bed, or use essential oils, such as lavender, camomile, patchouli and vetiver to ease my body into sleep.

Our sleep affects so many different areas of our life: our mood, our energy levels, happiness, how stressed we feel, our hormonal balance and even our skin. It is such a basic need and yet in today's frenetic lives, one that is so often cast very low down on our list of priorities.

THE HAYBARN SPA

Since I was very young I have had a curiosity to see and experience the world. Travel never ceases to inspire me; I learn, I meet people and I experience new and remarkable things. I am very fortunate in that being able to visit and explore other countries is still a huge part of my life and my travels continue to influence a lot of what I do.

I believe that taking time to nurture our mind is vital in restoring the balance so many of us lack in our lives. It reminds us of the need to be mindful in everything that we do.

For over 40 years I have been drawn back to India, captivated by its people, its vibrancy, its crafts and its colours, and the country has been a constant and unwavering source of inspiration for me.

It was an aspiration to learn yoga that first took me to India. Along with so many of my generation I was swept up in a desire to seek something beyond life as we knew it in the UK, something higher, more spiritual, and I found that at an ashram. Since then, India's yogic traditions in healing and well-being have continued to give me grounding and inspire me in so many ways.

But it was my encounter with Vettri Selvan over 12 years ago that was to spur me to do something that I think had always been growing in me, a wish to bring what I had learned about healing in India to Daylesford. Vettri was my yoga teacher throughout a stay there and when I met him I knew I'd met somebody very special and very spiritual. After each yoga session he would leave me with three thoughts for the day; they really moved me. I believe in things happening for reasons and after bumping into him a second time I felt that our paths had been destined to cross. I invited him to come back to England and set up what has become our Haybarn Spa.

Sometimes I think we were ahead of our time – too early in fact. The idea of creating a space simply to take care of your wellness, as opposed to your medical health via a doctor, seemed quite outlandish at the time. But for me it felt natural and innate. Part of being organic is about being kind to your body and a spa is rooted in the same belief: that we need to nurture ourselves and nurture each other. Our Haybarn Spa is a calming retreat; a place for meditation, yoga, Pilates, facial and massage treatments and relaxation. It is a place to take time for yourself, to

care for and be kind to yourself. All our treatments focus on healing and the work we do here is holistic; each therapist works with body, mind and spirit. Not only will you experience the physical effects of a massage – relaxed in your body and a release of tension in your muscles – you will feel calm, and the techniques used will release toxins in the body. Facials are designed to cleanse and nourish your skin; reflexology and lymphatic drainage will bring a radiant complexion but the type of massage brings you to a state of peace and deep relaxation.

My favourite treatment at the spa is a massage using hot and very cold jade stones and scented organic oils. Jade is a symbol of serenity and purity and the sensation of the two types of stone, applied with gentle pressure, is unlike anything I have ever experienced. Your eyes are closed so you have no expectation or sense of when or how the therapist will use each stone. Your body lets go and you allow your senses to be guided.

The massage is profoundly relaxing while at the same time energising and uplifting.

We live in a crazy, often stressful world but I feel that we are finally developing an awareness of the need to balance its freneticism and take time to care for ourselves and look after our mental, not just our physical, health. When I opened the spa, a massage was considered an excessive luxury and healing treatments, such as reflexology and reiki, were thought of as eccentric. Today many consider a massage to play an essential role in their self-care; it is a priority, rather than just an extravagant act of self-indulgence. People do take the time from their day to go to a spa. At the Haybarn that's simply the way it's always been.

POWERFUL BOTANY

Nature has so much to teach us and every day I am reminded of how powerful it is. It provides for us, it nurtures us and it tells us things. The variety of ingredients nature has to offer us, with their ability to heal, nourish and protect, is endless.

Our skin is our largest organ so it makes sense to me that what I put on my body is as nourishing as what goes into it. That is why I wanted to develop skincare and body products. I didn't want to be filling my body with the chemicals I was avoiding in my food, instead it was instinctive to look to nature and to the purest ingredients possible to feed my skin. But I also had to ensure that the products were made in an ecological and sustainable way, and of course that they would achieve visible results.

The Bamford skincare and body collections are made with naturally sourced and, wherever possible, certified organic ingredients. There are things that you simply can't guarantee as organic – sea salts or clays, for example – but our products contain high percentages of organic ingredients and all are tested and certified by the Soil Association, the UK's highest standard for organic beauty. Being under their guidance means that we have to prove that we're using the best ingredients but above all that we have consideration for ethical sourcing and that our products are sustainable and cruelty-free. Like the vegetables we grow in the garden, how we treat and process our ingredients is vital. We care for them, cold-pressing our oils to preserve their nutrients and goodness, and we use recycled materials to make our bottles and they themselves are all recyclable.

Everything we do at Bamford starts in nature, but the range is also very personal to me – led by the plants and herbs I love from my garden: geraniums, lavender, roses, rosehips, peppermint and rosemary. They provide beautiful fragrance but they are also all potent active ingredients. The scents and sensations of each collection are guided by how I feel at certain times of the day. In the morning I want to be uplifted and refreshed so I'll turn to peppermint and eucalyptus; they give me energy and a boost for the day. Geraniums also help to lift and balance mood as well as being cooling and deeply moisturising for my skin, while rosemary protects it against damage from any daytime pollution. And in the evening, if I'm having a bath, I want to feel soothed and calmed, my body relaxed and prepared for sleep, so I seek out lavender and camomile.

As a child, my grandmother used rosehip syrup a lot – for healing our cuts and scrapes – and I still believe in its power to restore the skin. Rosehip contains natural vitamin A, which is rejuvenating. We use it in our anti-ageing range as it visibly reduces the appearance of wrinkles and fine lines.

The farm also provides me with references and guidance. Our orchard of heritage apples inspired us to look into the properties of fruit enzymes and we were delighted to discover that apples have wonderful benefits for the skin; their malic acid helps resurface it. And our annual crop of strawberries steered us towards the fruit's seeds, which are hydrating and nourishing for the skin.

WELL-BEING BOOSTS

I believe that looking after our well-being is a holistic process but above all one that is unique to each of us. What works for one may not suit another, and the same goes for the foods we eat.

As I've said, I don't follow any kind of philosophy when it comes to food – I believe in eating a balanced diet with a range of nutrients, ideally organically grown or produced. Nevertheless, I do believe there are times when certain ingredients can be used to help give your body a particular boost or remedy an imbalance. Over the next few pages are recipes for those times. Liquid-based, these juices, broths and tonics are particularly rich in vitamins and minerals designed to heal, soothe or revitalise.

There has been a lot of talk in the UK about turmeric recently. The Indians have been using this root for centuries for its anti-inflammatory properties and it's an ingredient I learned about on a visit there years ago. Since then I have been drinking a shot of juiced turmeric and ginger whenever I feel like my body is under the weather or heading for a cold. It instantly lifts me and gives me a boost of energy and clarity.

It is hard for your body to fully assimilate the effects of turmeric unless you serve it with a portion of good fat and black pepper so the turmeric milk drink overleaf is one of the best recipes to ensure that you are absorbing it effectively.

Turmeric does have to come from abroad because it can't be grown in this country but we source ours extremely carefully, as sustainably as we can. We know which producers it comes from and ensure it is shipped to us by a means that creates no additional carbon footprint.

I've also previously talked about stocks, or 'bone broths' as they're now commonly referred to, as they're something I grew up making with my mother every week. Beyond the fact that for me there is nothing like the flavour that can be extracted from simmering bones for hours, stocks are also extremely good for us. The collagen and cartilage leached into the water contain glycoproteins, which are the building blocks of our own joints. The gelatine in the broths helps keep our skin plump and our hair glossy, while the nourishing minerals, fats, glucosamine and amino acids are easy to digest and help seal and repair the gut lining. If you are struggling with your digestion and you suffer pain or bloating this is an easy way to soothe and improve it – in one simple, sustainable, nourishing cup.

Turmeric and tamarind tonic

I'd suggest wearing rubber gloves when you prepare your turmeric, and be mindful of your surfaces – it stains everything a bright yellow.

MAKES 700ML

250g fresh turmeric root, peeled and chopped
1 litre mineral water
125ml tamarind paste
125g light brown palm sugar

Combine the fresh turmeric with the mineral water and pour into a pan. Add the tamarind paste and palm sugar and bring to the boil. Reduce the heat and simmer for 30 minutes.

Strain through a sieve into a clean jug while still warm and leave to cool. Once cooled chill in the fridge before serving.

Golden turmeric milk

If you're experiencing any aches, pains or sleepless nights during the cold winter months a warming cup of this magnesium-rich comforting drink should soothe and reduce the inflammation in your body.

SERVES 1

300ml full-fat milk (or unsweetened almond milk)
1 tsp honey
4 cardamom pods, lightly crushed
1 tsp grated fresh turmeric
1 cinnamon stick
pinch of black pepper
2 slices of fresh ginger

Heat the milk in a small pan with all the other ingredients over a medium heat. Stir to dissolve the honey and boil briefly before turning off the heat. Leave to infuse for 2 minutes.

Strain the milk to remove the whole spices and leave to cool a little. Serve while still warm.

WELL-BEING • EACH JUICE SERVES 2

Full of vitamins and nutrients, each of these juices has a health-boosting property. The Balanced juice is rich in chlorophyll, vitamin C and potassium, which is good for balancing the nervous system. Bright gives you a good dose of vitamin A, which contributes to good eye health and healthy skin. And Bold will give your brain a boost and helps to reduce fatigue.

b Balanced

1 cucumber, chopped
1 apple, cored and chopped
3 celery sticks, chopped
handful of spinach
juice of ½ lemon
small handful of parsley

b Bright

200g carrots (about 3), ends trimmed and chopped
1 apple, cored and chopped
3 celery sticks, chopped
thumb-sized piece of fresh ginger, peeled and chopped
juice of 1 lemon

b Bold

juice of 1 large orange, pips removed
1 raw beetroot, peeled and chopped
2 apples, cored and chopped
thumb-sized piece of turmeric root, peeled and chopped

Pass all the ingredients through a juicer and serve. To make any of these into a smoothie, halve the ingredients and whizz in a high-speed blender with 100ml water until combined, adding more water if desired.

WELL-BEING • EACH BROTH MAKES 2–2.5 LITRES

In the past few years, the boiling of bones to make broths has become popular again, and I'm delighted to see it. Not only does it mean that we are reviving a tradition that was second nature to previous generations, we're being mindful of the way we eat – not wasting a part of an animal that has been slaughtered. The cooking time for these broths might seem long but extracting the nutrients from the bones takes time and the longer you boil them, the better for you they will be. Use the broths to cook rice, quinoa or other grains, or make a quick meal by serving them on their own or topped with seasonal vegetables – either crunchy and raw or lightly steamed.

Beef bone broth

2.5kg beef bones
2 carrots, roughly chopped
2 small onions, roughly chopped
1 leek, roughly chopped
2 celery sticks, roughly chopped

1 garlic clove, finely chopped
2 tsp vegetable oil
2 tbsp tomato purée
10g thyme sprigs
5.5 litres cold water

Preheat the oven to 200°C/gas 6.

Place the bones in a roasting tray and roast for 1 hour.

Put the vegetable oil into a large stockpot, add the carrot, onion, leek and celery and cook over a medium heat until golden brown, then the garlic and allow it to colour, then add the tomato purée and cook for a further 5 minutes. Add the thyme and water and then the roasted bones, ensuring none of the fat from the roasting tray goes into the liquid. Bring to a simmer and then skim off all the fat. Leave to simmer for a minimum of 10 hours, skimming constantly. Do not let it boil rapidly or the stock will go cloudy. Pass the stock through a fine sieve and chill, removing any remaining fat from the surface before using. Store in the fridge for up to 3 days or freeze for up to 3 months.

Chicken bone broth

1 white onion, roughly chopped
2 celery sticks, roughly chopped
1 leek, roughly chopped
½ fennel bulb, roughly chopped

1 garlic clove, finely chopped
1.1kg chicken bones/carcass
10g thyme sprigs
5 litres cold water

Put the vegetables into a large stockpot or saucepan, add the chicken bones, thyme and water, bring to a simmer then skim off all the fat. Leave to simmer for a minimum of 10 hours, skimming constantly. Do not let it boil rapidly or the stock will go cloudy. Pass the stock through a fine sieve and and chill, removing any remaining fat from the surface before using. Store in the fridge for up to 3 days or freeze for up to 3 months.

TIME FOR TEA

The English are often mocked for believing that a cup of tea solves all manner of ill but I too am firmly of that belief. I use teas to cleanse, energise, revive, heal and restore.

I like different teas at different times of the day or just depending on how I'm feeling: an energising tea, such as green tea, to start the day; a cleansing tea, such as nettle leaf, peppermint or fennel, to aid digestion; a refreshing tea, perhaps served cold, such as elderflower, in the summer; and I love sleepy, relaxing teas, such as camomile or lavender, before I go to bed.

I've learned a lot about teas and their impact on our bodies through travel. I love the care and the ritual that surrounds the making of tea in Japan. Like their approach to cooking there's such a profound respect for the ingredient. Despite being open to every kind of tea, matcha was one I wasn't really able to embrace or enjoy until I went to Japan and had it served as it should be.

Matcha is a green tea that has been steamed, dried and ground into a powder. When you drink it you're consuming the whole tea leaf and therefore, unlike with other teas, you receive all of its nutrients. Alongside the vitamins and minerals found in the tea, matcha is thought to benefit us in many other ways. The tea will calm our minds yet energise our bodies and stimulate our concentration, and it is also thought to lower our cholesterol..

To make matcha, the tea leaves are harvested exactly 66 days after the spring equinox and only the first three leaves of each branch are picked by hand. Often the plants are shaded when they begin to bud so that they are not exposed to direct sunlight. It is a very precious ingredient and as such it merits the attention and respect the Japanese afford it when preparing it. I discovered that I was making mine the wrong way, burning the precious powder by using water that was boiling, and not whisking the tea with the bamboo whisk as tradition calls for. The traditions aren't just part of a ceremony or spectacle; they are all necessary stages in guaranteeing the perfect flavour; the perfect cup of tea.

END NOTE

Life on a farm follows a rhythm. There is the sowing and harvesting, the new life to be celebrated, the new season's rituals, produce and festivities to be revelled in. These punctuate the year, guiding and steadying us as we meet its joys and face its challenges.

When the snowdrops poke their heads out of the ground to greet spring's morning light, or the sun sinks lower in the sky and the woolly jumpers, wellingtons and chill in the air mark the start of autumn days, the shift in the season is a reminder to me of our connection to this earth and the debt we owe it in providing for us. Life on a farm ties us to nature but it also throws us at its mercy – with all that that may bring.

My hope with this book is that it might inspire you: to grow some seeds of your own; to make a jam, stew or stock from scratch; to try a seasonal ingredient you've not tasted; to forage in your local hedgerows and pick your own fruits; or simply to nurture your body and mind in the way that feels right to you. I hope that it may also remind you of why we need to look after what we have: to nourish and care for our soil, our land and our planet, in order that we are not the last to enjoy its riches. Thanks to Daylesford, the work that we do here and the produce and products we offer, I feel that in our own small way we are celebrating those riches, sharing nature's gifts with others, nurturing this small corner of the Cotswolds as best we can, as well as giving back a little of what we take to produce what we do.

But life on a working farm, particularly an organic one, is also a stark and daily reminder to me of how precious and precarious life is and how vulnerable we are to nature's ebbs and flows. I am very lucky to have been given the life and opportunities I have. Every day nature reminds me to be grateful for those privileges and to celebrate all that it gives us. We only have one chance at this life and have been blessed with so much; let's make sure that we nurture what we have, to ensure that future generations can share in those blessings too.

ACKNOWLEDGEMENTS

This book is a celebration of the work our team at Daylesford and Bamford carries out every day and it would not have been possible without their commitment and passion to make the farm and everything we do a reality. I owe them all enormous thanks.

But in writing this book, I am particularly grateful for the help and contribution of certain people who have given me their time and support so generously.

A very big thank you to Sophie Richardson, for your dedication, attention to detail and tireless enthusiasm for the project. It would not have been possible without all your hard work, vision and coordination.

To Amy Devine, for your beautiful design, creative direction and for bringing the farm to life on the page so elegantly. It is always a pleasure working with you; thank you for your humour and endless hard work.

Adam Caisley, our very talented chef wrote the wonderful recipes for the book, many of which are old family favourites or dishes Anthony and I have come to adore thanks to his creativity. Thank you for endlessly delighting us with your talents and inspiring me with your hard work and love for good food. A big thank you also to Gaven Fuller for all your recipe contributions, particularly for those with a focus on well-being. And with thanks to Annabel Briggs for reading and testing all the recipes.

To Martin Morrell: we have worked together for years now and yet I continue to be in awe of your talents and ability to see the extraordinary in the ordinary. Thank you for capturing our world so beautifully from behind your lens.

Thank you also to Keiko Oikawa and Linda Berlin for your graceful, inspiring images of the recipes, and Rosalind Atkinson, Britt Willoughby Dyer and Andrew Montgomery for the striking photography that also graces these pages.

Heartfelt thanks to my publisher Square Peg, in particular to Rowan Yapp, Shabana Cho and Susannah Otter.

And finally to Imogen Fortes, for helping me translate my vision and world into words on the page with sensitivity, care, insight and understanding. I will forever be grateful we were introduced.

A

abattoir 220
Aberdeen Angus cattle 47, 219
Aïoli, saffron 136
almonds: Plum and bitter almond jam 202
anchovies: Raw artichoke with anchovy and caper dressing 159
animal welfare 43–5, 220
antiques 97
apples 189, 198, 232, 281
    b Balanced juice 287
    b Bold juice 287
    b Bright juice 287
    Beetroot, apple and ginger chutney 201
    Matcha sour cocktail 77
    Onion and cider soup with rarebit 232
    Orchard punch 76
    Slow-cooked pigs' cheeks, turnip, apple, hazelnuts and celeriac mash 243
Artichoke, raw with anchovy and caper dressing 159
artisan craftsmen 110
asparagus 121, 126, 139
    Asparagus risotto with wild garlic pesto 139
    Asparagus with salsa verde 127
    Dressed crab with shaved asparagus 132
    Leg of hogget with parsley crust, greens and buttered potatoes 142–3
    Purple and white asparagus with purple sprouting broccoli and hollandaise 128
autumn 189

B

b Balanced juice 287
b Bold juice 287
b Bright juice 287
bacon
    Baywell tartiflette 204
    Roast cod and Jerusalem artichokes in smoked bacon broth 207
    Roast salmon, peas, bacon and braised Little Gem 165
bakery, the 33–4
Bamford
    clothing range 98–111
    skincare and body collection 281
barbecues 169
Baywell cheese 31
    Baywell tartiflette 204
beans 121
    Spring green minestrone 131
beef
    Beef bone broth 288
    Beef shin stew with Marmite and Cheddar dumplings 245
    Bone marrow and barley risotto 238
    Oxtail and kimchi broth 288
    Oxtail stew with mash and cabbage 222
beekeeping 182, 213
beetroot
    b Bold juice 287
    Beetroot, apple and ginger chutney 201
Beluga lentil, squash and wild rice 196
berries 215
    Chicken liver pâté with pickled blackberries and red cabbage 193
    Léoube rosé jelly with summer berries 179
blackberries 193, 215
    Chicken liver pâté with pickled blackberries and red cabbage 193
bluebells 148
'bone broths' 283
    Beef bone 288
    Chicken bone 288
Bone marrow and barley risotto 238
bread
    Honey, fig and walnut sourdough 41
    Onion and cider soup with rarebit 232
    Potato and thyme sourdough 38
    sourdough starter 38
broccoli 121
    Chestnut bubble and squeak 260
    Leg of hogget with parsley crust, greens and buttered potatoes 142–3
    Purple and white asparagus with purple sprouting broccoli and hollandaise 128
    Sprouting broccoli pizza 75
    Winter greens 235
broths, see bone broths
Brussels sprouts 227
    Chestnut bubble and squeak 260
bulgur wheat: Summer tabbouleh 162
buttermilk 26
butternut squash: Beluga lentil, squash and wild rice 196
button cuff sweater, the 104

C

cabbage 121
    Chestnut bubble and squeak 260
    Pickled blackberries and red cabbage with chicken liver pâté 193
    Oxtail stew with mash and cabbage 222
    Winter greens 235
camomile 281
capers
    Grilled sardines with tomato and caper sauce and saffron aïoli 136
    Raw artichoke with anchovy and caper dressing 159
carrots: b Bright juice 287
cattle 29, 43, 47
cauliflower
    Piccalilli 202
    Raw cauliflower and black quinoa with spiced pumpkin seed dressing 194
    Winter greens 235
celeriac: Slow-cooked pigs' cheeks, turnip, apple, hazelnuts and celeriac mash 243
celery 227
    b Balanced juice 287
    b Bright juice 287
Château Léoube 173–7
Cheddar
    Beef shin stew with Marmite and Cheddar dumplings 245
    Daylesford Cheddar 31, 227
    Onion and cider soup with rarebit 232
cheese 26, 29, 30, 204, 227
    Adlestrop 31
    Artemis Greek-Style 31
    Baywell 31, 204
    Baywell tartiflette 204
    Beef shin stew with Marmite and Cheddar dumplings 245
    Bledington Blue 31
    Daylesford Blue 31
    Daylesford Cheddar 31, 227
    Double Gloucester 31
    Foscot 31
    Mont d'Or 227, 232
    Onion and cider soup with rarebit 232
    Single Gloucester 26, 29, 31
    Single Gloucester pizza 75
cheese-making 26
Chestnut bubble and squeak 260
chefs 60
chicken
    Chicken and barley broth 288
    Chicken bone broth 288
    Chicken liver pâté with pickled blackberries and red cabbage 193
    Flat-iron chicken and kale 236
chickens 50
Christmas 253–9
    making a Christmas wreath 256
Chutney, beetroot, apple and ginger 201
cider 189, 232
    Onion and cider soup with rarebit 232
clementines: Egg custard tart with clementines, ginger and pecans 246
cocktails, see drinks
cod, roast, and Jerusalem artichokes in smoked bacon broth 207

conscious living 16
Consommé, tomato 154
cookery school, the 79–83
courgettes
    Spring green minestrone 131
    Winter greens 235
Crab, dressed with shaved asparagus 132
creamery, the 25–6
cucumber
    b Balanced juice 287
    Cucumber salad 160
    English garden cocktail 77
    Matcha sour cocktail 77
    Piccalilli 202

D

Daylesford cottages 91–5
Daylesford garden 85–9
Dressed crab with shaved asparagus 132
dressings
    Anchovy and caper 159
    Spiced pumpkin seed 194
drinks
    b Balanced juice 287
    b Bold juice 287
    b Bright juice 287
    English garden 77
    Golden turmeric milk 284
    Matcha sour 77
    Orchard punch 76
    Pea shoot sour 77
    Summer cup 166
    Turmeric tamarind tonic 284
    Vitamin tonic 76
dumplings, Marmite and Cheddar 245

E

Easter 141
eggs 50
    Egg custard tart with clementines, ginger and pecans 246
    English garden cocktail 77
eucalyptus 281

F

farm shops, the 63–7
figs: Honey, fig and walnut sourdough loaf 41
fish and seafood 165
    Dressed crab with shaved asparagus 132
    Grilled sardines with tomato and caper sauce and saffron aïoli 136
    Jersey royal salad with smoked trout and tarragon mayonnaise 135
    Roast cod and Jerusalem artichokes in smoked bacon broth 207
    Roast salmon, peas, bacon and braised Little Gem 165
Flat-iron chicken and kale 236
flowers 87–9
food waste 15, 238
foraging 81–3, 88, 253
France 156, 173–7
Friesians 47
Fung, Spencer 67

G

game 208, 227
    Roast partridge with lentils, sausage and kale 208
    Venison ragu with pappardelle 240
garlic 121
    Asparagus risotto with wild garlic pesto 139
    Garlic oil 162
geraniums 281
gin
    English garden cocktail 77
    Pea shoot sour cocktail 77
ginger
    b Bright juice 287
    Beetroot, apple and ginger chutney 201
    Egg custard tart with clementines, ginger and pecans 246
    Panna cotta with poached rhubarb, blood orange and ginger 146
    Steamed ginger pudding and poached rhubarb 249
    Vitamin tonic 76
Golden turmeric milk 284
gooseberries 153
grapefruit: Vitamin tonic 76
Grilled sardines with tomato and caper sauce and saffron aïoli 136

H

Haybarn Spa 275–81
hazelnuts: Slow-cooked pig's cheeks, turnip, apple and celeriac mash 243
hedgerow fruits 215
herbs 162
heritage orchard, the 198
Heritage tomato salad with tapenade 156
hogget 142
    Leg of hogget with parsley crust, greens and buttered potatoes 142–3
holistic living 12–15, 283
Hollandaise 128
honey 182, 213
    Honey, fig and walnut sourdough loaf 41
    Honey parfait with poached pears, honeycomb and lemon curd 213
    Honeycomb 213
    Vitamin tonic 76

I

ikat weave 102
India 102, 253, 277
ingredients 58
Italy 104

J

jam, plum and bitter almond 202
Japan 100, 110, 290
jelly, Léoube rosé with summer berries 179
Jersey royal salad with smoked trout and tarragon mayonnaise 135
jerusalem artichokes 231
    Jerusalem artichoke soup 231
    Roast cod and Jerusalem artichokes in smoked bacon broth 207
juices
    b Balanced 287
    b Bold 287
    b Bright 287

K

kale
    Flat-iron chicken and kale 236
    Roast partridge with lentils, sausage and kale 208
    Summer tabbouleh 162
    Winter greens 235
kefir 26
Kerry Hill sheep 109
kimchi. Oxtail and kimchi broth 288

L

lamb 142
    Leg of hogget with parsley crust, greens and buttered potatoes 142–3
lambing 121
lavender 218
Leg of hogget with parsley crust, greens and buttered potatoes 142–3
Legbar hens 50
lemon curd 213

lentils
    Beluga lentil, squash and wild rice 196
    Roast partridge with lentils, sausage and kale 208
Léoube estate 173–7
Léoube rosé jelly with summer berries 179
lettuce: Roast salmon, peas, bacon and braised Little Gem 165
living from the land 15
loganberries: Léoube rosé jelly with summer berries 179

M

market garden, the 53–5
Marmite and Cheddar dumplings 245
matcha 290
    Matcha sour cocktail 77
mayonnaise
    Saffron aïoli 136
    Tarragon mayonnaise 135
meditation 271
milk 26
    Golden turmeric milk 284
Minestrone, spring green 131
mint
    English garden cocktail 77
    Matcha sour cocktail 77
mocktails, see drinks
mushrooms: Venison ragu with pappardelle 240

N

New Year 264
nuts
    Egg custard tart with clementines, ginger and pecans 246
    Honey, fig and walnut sourdough 41
    Slow-cooked pig's cheeks, turnip, apple, hazelnuts and celeriac mash 243

O

Old Gloucester cattle 29, 47
Old Spot bar, the 71–2
olives 177
    Heritage tomato salad with tapenade 156
    olive oil 177
Onion and cider soup with rarebit 232
oranges
    b Bold juice 287
    Panna cotta with poached rhubarb, blood orange and ginger 146
Orchard punch 76
organic farming 45, 55
organic food 12
Oxtail stew with mash and cabbage 222

P

packaging 15
Panna cotta with poached rhubarb, blood orange and ginger 146
Parfait, honey with poached pears, honeycomb and lemon curd 213
partridge 208, 227
    Roast partridge with lentils, sausage and kale 208
pasta: Venison ragu with pappardelle 240
Pâté, chicken liver with pickled blackberries and red cabbage 193
Pea shoot sour cocktail 77
pearl barley
    Bone marrow and barley risotto 238
    Chicken and barley broth 288
pears: Honey parfait with poached pears, honeycomb and lemon curd 213
peas 121
    Pea shoot sour cocktail 77
    Radishes, fresh peas, butter, salt 128
    Roast salmon, peas, bacon and braised Little Gem 165
    Spring green minestrone 131
pecans
    Egg custard tart with clementines, ginger and pecans 246
    Flat-iron chicken and kale 236
peppermint 281
pesto
    Asparagus risotto with wild garlic pesto 139
    Sprouting broccoli pizza 75
Piccalilli 202
pizzas
    Single Gloucester pizza 75
    Spelt pizza dough 72
    Sprouting broccoli pizza 75
    Traditional pizza dough 72
plums
    Plum and bitter almond jam 202
    Rice pudding with poached plums 210
pomegranate: Orchard Punch 76
pork
    Slow-cooked pigs' cheeks, turnip, apple, hazelnuts and celeriac mash 243
    see also bacon; sausages
potatoes 121, 135
    Baywell tartiflette 204
    Chestnut bubble and squeak 260
    Jersey royal salad with smoked trout and tarragon mayonnaise 135
    Leg of hogget with parsley crust, greens and buttered potatoes 142–3
    Oxtail stew with mash and cabbage 222
    Potato and thyme sourdough loaf 38
    Roast salmon, peas, bacon and braised Little Gem 165
pottery 110
preserves
    Beetroot, apple and ginger chutney 201
    Piccalilli 202
    Plum and bitter almond jam 202
Provence 173–7
Pudding, steamed ginger and poached rhubarb 249
Purple and white asparagus with purple sprouting broccoli and hollandaise 128

Q

quinoa
    Raw cauliflower and black quinoa with spiced pumpkin seed dressing 194
    Summer tabbouleh 162

R

radishes, fresh peas, butter, salt 128
ragu, venison with pappardelle 240
raspberries: Léoube rosé jelly with summer berries 179
Raw artichoke with anchovy and caper dressing 159
Raw cauliflower and black quinoa with spiced pumpkin seed dressing 194
red deer 219
rhubarb
    Panna cotta with poached rhubarb, blood orange and ginger 146
    Steamed ginger pudding and poached rhubarb 249
rice
    Asparagus risotto with wild garlic pesto 139
    Beluga lentil, squash and wild rice 196
    Bone marrow and barley risotto 238
    Rice pudding with poached plums 210
risotto
    Asparagus risotto with wild garlic pesto 139
    Bone marrow and barley risotto 238
Roast cod and Jerusalem artichokes in smoked bacon broth 207
Roast partridge with lentils, sausage and kale 208
Roast salmon, peas, bacon and braised Little Gem 165

rocket: Spring green minestrone 131
rosehips 281
rosemary 281
Ryland sheep 109

S

Saffron aïoli 136
salads
    Beluga lentil, squash and wild rice 196
    Cucumber salad 160
    Flat-iron chicken and kale 236
    Heritage tomato salad with tapenade 156
    Jersey royal salad with smoked trout and tarragon mayonnaise 135
    Raw artichoke with anchovy and caper dressing 159
    Raw cauliflower and black quinoa with spiced pumpkin seed dressing 194
    Summer tabbouleh 162
    Winter greens 235
salmon: Roast salmon, peas, bacon and braised Little Gem 165
Salsa verde 127
sardines 136
    Grilled sardines with tomato and caper sauce and saffron aioli 136
sauces
    Hollandaise 128
    Salsa verde 127
    Tapenade 156
    Tomato and caper sauce 136
    Wild garlic pesto 139
sausages: Roast partridge with lentils, sausage and kale 208
Scotland, 104
seafood, see fish and seafood
sheep 109
Simnel cake 141
Single Gloucester 26, 29, 31
    Single Gloucester pizza 75
sleep 272
sloes 215
Slow-cooked pigs' cheeks, turnip, apple, hazelnuts and celeriac mash 243
Smith, Richard 45, 47
snowdrops 123–5
soups
    Jerusalem artichoke soup 231
    Spring green minestrone 131
    Tomato consommé 154
sourdough 38
    Honey, fig and walnut sourdough 41
    Potato and thyme sourdough 38
    sourdough starter 38
South Devon cows 47
spinach: Spring green minestrone 131
spring 121
Spring green minestrone 131
Sprouting broccoli pizza 75
Staffordshire 219–20
Steamed ginger pudding and poached rhubarb 249
summer 153
Summer cup 166
Summer tabbouleh 162
swede: Chestnut bubble and squeak 260

T

Tabbouleh, summer 162
table dressing 170, 180, 191, 229, 259
tamarind: Turmeric tamarind tonic 284
Tapenade 156
Tart, Egg custard with clementines, ginger and pecans 246
Tartiflette, Baywell 204
tayberries: Léoube rosé jelly with summer berries 179
tea 290
    Matcha sour cocktail 77
tomatoes
    Grilled sardines with tomato and caper sauce and saffron aïoli 136
    Heritage tomato salad with tapenade 156
    Single Gloucester pizza 75
    Summer tabbouleh 162
    Tomato consommé 154
trout: Jersey royal salad with smoked trout and tarragon mayonnaise 135
turmeric 283
    b Bold juice 287
    Golden turmeric milk 284
    Turmeric tamarind tonic 284
turnips: Slow-cooked pigs' cheeks, turnip, apple, hazelnuts and celeriac mash 243

V

venison 227
    Venison ragu with pappardelle 240
Vettri Selvan 271, 277
Vitamin Tonic 76
vodka: Matcha Sour cocktail 77

W

'wabi-sabi' 100
walnuts 41, 189
    Honey, fig and walnut sourdough 41
well-being 267–83
Wild garlic pesto 139
Wild Rabbit, The 112–17
wine
    Léoube rosé jelly with summer berries 179
    Summer cup 166
    wine-making 175–7
Winter greens 235
wool 109
Wootton 219–20

Y

yoga 271, 277
yoghurt 26

EBURY PRESS

UK | USA | Canada | Ireland | Australia
India | New Zealand | South Africa

Ebury Press is part of the Penguin Random House group of companies whose addresses can be found at global.penguinrandomhouse.com

Penguin Random House UK
One Embassy Gardens, 8 Viaduct Gardens, London SW11 7BW

penguin.co.uk
global.penguinrandomhouse.com

First published by Square Peg in 2018
This edition published by Ebury Press in 2025
1

Copyright © Carole Bamford 2018, 2025

Reportage photography:
Martin Morrell pages 4, 8, 10, 13-14, 17-18, 22, 27-28, 36, 42, 44-48, 50-51, 56, 59, 61-62, 64, 66-69, 82-84, 90, 92-98, 102, 106, 108-109, 115-121, 140, 148, 150-153, 168, 170, 174, 176-177, 180, 183-188, 199-200, 203, 214, 216-221, 224, 226, 228, 250, 254-255, 262, 265-268, 270-276, 278-280, 282, 291-294, 298, end papers, back cover (portrait).
Keiko Oikawa pages 60, 73, 83 (gnocchi), 86-89, 122, 123-124, 144, 146, 189 (squash), 190, 252, 257, 258, back cover (tabletop).
Andrew Montgomery pages 24, 27, 30, 32, 35, 70, 73, 101, 109 (yarn), 112.
Rosalind Atkinson front cover, pages 6, 256.
Sarah Maingot pages 54, 143, 227.
Britt Wilder pages 52, 66 (Chelsea Garden Room), 188 (apples).
Gavin White pages 176-177 (colour), 296.
Neil Watson page 78.
Matthew Gorman page 80.
Neil Davenport page 103.
Tomoko Meguro page 111.
Lionel Bouffier page 172.

Recipe photography: Keiko Oikawa (except pages 223 and 261 by Martin Morrell)
Food and prop styling: Linda Berlin
Design: Amy Devine
Recipes: Adam Caisley and Gaven Fuller
Illustrations: Hugo Guinness
Illustrated map: Joy Gosney

The moral right of the author has been asserted.

No part of this book may be used or reproduced in any manner for the purpose of training artificial intelligence technologies or systems. In accordance with Article 4(3) of the DSM Directive 2019/790, Penguin Random House expressly reserves this work from the text and data mining exception.

Colour origination by Altaimage Ltd
Printed and bound in Italy by LEGO SpA

The authorised representative in the EEA is Penguin Random House Ireland, Morrison Chambers, 32 Nassau Street, Dublin D02 YH68.

A CIP catalogue record for this book is available from the British Library

ISBN 9781529985450

Penguin Random House is committed to a sustainable future for our business, our readers and our planet. This book is made from Forest Stewardship Council® certified paper.